CU

The Ben Fixman Story:

FROM THE GHETTO TO THE GOLD

The Ben Fixman Story:
FROM THE GHETTO TO THE GOLD

AS TOLD TO DONALD ROTH
2009

Published by Artful Tale LLC
With special thanks to Richard S. Beldner for his input into major sections of
this book. Rick has been my close friend and associate for nearly 40 years.

Graphic design and layout: Cathy Wood, www.cathywoodbookdesign.com
Cover illustration: Mike Eckhard of Bream Marketing Group
Photo research and coordinator: Christy Marshall
Printed and manufactured in the United States by Sheridan Books, Inc.

CU The letters CU used throughout the book represent the
symbol for copper from the Periodic Table of Elements.

For my family and friends

CONTENTS

With Jewish engineering, you either solve the problem or you starve to death.

—Ben Fixman

THE BEN FIXMAN STORY:
FROM THE GHETTO TO THE GOLD

From a dirt-poor beginning in a dingy St. Louis ghetto hustling newspapers to whores and pimps at age 7, I grew up the son of a widowed, Yiddish-speaking Russian immigrant mother and became a self-educated entrepreneur. I created a New York Stock Exchange Company and revolutionized the American scrap metals industry by developing an anti-pollution process decades before "going green" became the rage. I successfully sued AT&T in a giant anti-trust action, and kept my cancer-stricken wife alive for more than 14½ years after her doctors told her she had just 90 days to live. I became a close acquaintance of the leaders of Israel and gave away millions in philanthropy. I would have given away even more *gelt* (money), but I never could resist the lure of the crap tables in Las Vegas.

We were the poorest family in the ghetto. Very often we didn't have a dime to buy a loaf of bread so we bought it on credit. When I didn't have three cents to buy an ice cream cone, a drug store owner let me lick the insides of his discarded ice cream containers. A friendly neighbor gave me her barbecue bones to suck on after she had eaten them for dinner. And what a treat they were—especially if there were a few slivers of meat left.

My story only could have happened in America where endless opportunities abound despite the current recession, but only if you come to the table equipped with "big balls" and a driving determination to succeed.

This memoir is an exact retelling of my life. Every word in it is true. In the book, I have tried to create a bit of humor by inserting a few Yiddish expressions. I am 84 years old now and still speak perfect Yiddish, a language I learned as part of my heritage of being a proud Jew.

If I may have misspelled a Yiddish word or phrase or dropped in a profane word now and then, I apologize. But for me to sanitize this book by eliminating all the salty language would have watered down the truth and been an absolute disservice to my friends and business associates. I wanted this book to replicate exactly how its characters spoke—to be as authentic, realistic and as genuine as was humanly possible. So, once again, pardon the profanity, but that's the way it was.

I have one more apology. I want to say I'm sorry to my Hebrew School teacher who rapped me over the knuckles with a ruler because I wasn't paying attention in class. I jumped up and punched Rabbi Becker smack in the middle of his beard. What did I know? I was only 12 years old. Rabbi, wherever you are, you have my apologies. I even forgive you for kicking my ass right out of Hebrew School. But a pious Jew who owned a junkyard in the ghetto saw to it that I was indeed *bar mitzvahed*. He took me to a *shul* (synagogue) one Thursday morning, said some mysterious words in Hebrew and declared that I was a *bar mitzvah* boy. And that's how I became a man.

When I was young, horses and carts were still a common sight in my neighborhood.
MISSOURI HISTORY MUSEUM, ST. LOUIS

Regarding my business endeavors, I would like to give my personal thanks to the dedicated team of "metals people" who helped me build Diversified. Without their efforts and creativity, none of this would ever have happened. I am forever in their debt.

A final thought: My success story had its roots in the last century in an economic time far different from the deep recession currently affecting our nation. But the business lessons I learned well over a generation ago still remain relevant—no matter the present state of the economy.

I firmly believe that you can still make it big in America. But you must have an unwavering belief in yourself; you must be willing to literally work your ass off; you must hire top talent and reward them monetarily; and you must create a workplace environment where your people eagerly look forward to coming to work each and every day.

If you are capable of doing all of that, there is absolutely no limit on how great your success will be.

And never forget that you are truly blessed to be living in the greatest nation on earth—a true "melting pot" that permitted my childhood dream of becoming a success to be realized; a nation where boundless opportunities STILL exist every day for men and women of every race, religion or creed to make their mark in this world, no matter how humble their beginnings.

As I've often heard said: "ONLY IN AMERICA."

September 24, 2009

CHAPTER ONE

THE NIGHTMARE OF THE GHETTO

I grew up smack in the middle of the Great American Depression in the worst ghetto in all of St. Louis.

As a fatherless child, I suffered from never-ending poverty and the pangs of hunger; anti-Semites screamed venomous slurs at me; huge rats ate through the walls of our tiny flat at night and attacked our family. My mother, Rose, was an immigrant from Russia who gave me no love, kisses or hugs, but beat the hell out of me regularly, using a right hand that could have cold cocked Joe Louis or Rocky Marciano.

I never had a childhood. None at all. At the tender age of 7, I was already hustling newspapers on freezing street corners and servicing a paper route teeming with whores and pimps. (The whores, by the way, were great tippers. If I delivered a *St. Louis Globe-Democrat* or a *Post-Dispatch* that cost two cents, more often than not, they would toss me a nickel and say: "Kid, keep the change.")

I was born January 21, 1925, in an old flat at 1824 Carr Street, right next to Willy Wexler's junkyard. Assisted by a midwife named "Mrs. Diamond," my mother delivered a very large son named Ben who checked into this world at a whopping 10 pounds.

The Fixman family consisted of my stern mother, Rose; my father, Bernard, a Russian-born junk dealer (whom I never knew because he died of complications of bladder surgery when I was just 18 months old); my brother, Hymie; and three sisters: Celia, Nina and Martha. I was the

EVEN ONE OF THE TOUGHEST GUYS IN THE GHETTO, JACKIE DICKER, WOULDN'T TAKE ME ON. JACKIE LATER WENT ON TO WIN THE 1946 GOLDEN GLOVES TITLE AT 126 POUNDS. HE TURNED PRO AND WON 16 FIGHTS IN A ROW BEFORE HIS WIFE MADE HIM QUIT THE RING.

youngest in the family, a child destined to end up with the nickname of "Benny the Fix"—a tag the neighborhood kids hung on me because I quickly learned to use my fists to protect myself. I never went looking for trouble in the ghetto, but if I had to duke it out, I made a habit of slugging the other guy first with three hard punches before he could even lay one hand on me. I made a name for myself as a duker, a kid you didn't want to challenge or fuck with. In all my ghetto fights, I never lost one.

Since my father had no life insurance, the family was destitute after his death, and we were forced to suffer the *shonda* (Yiddish for shame) of temporarily going on relief. But all through those long and bitter ghetto years on Carr Street—with little food in our bellies and often no coal in the furnace to heat our flat—we were sustained by our faith as an Orthodox Jewish family and by working our tails off to put some food on the table.

My mother, a street-smart woman, spoke only broken English. (When she decided to become a U.S. citizen, she learned the language in a year.) She worked out a deal with our landlord whereby she collected the rent from the three black families in our building, and in return, we were allowed to live rent-free. It was like a gift from God. It made the difference. Without it, who knows where our struggling family would have ended up? Out on the street, that's where.

To stay alive, all six of us worked for slave wages. When she could find work, my mother was a domestic toiling away for $1 for a FULL day cleaning someone's home or apartment. If she got lucky, she might make

$2 for a full day's work. Hymie made $6 a week at Ace Electric; Celia, the big breadwinner in the family, earned $8 a week selling vegetables at the food center in the Biddle Market; Martha got $5 a week working at a dry goods store on Franklin Avenue, while Nina also got $5 a week at another dry goods store. I made 35 cents a day peddling newspapers from 3 p.m. to 7 p.m. In all, our total family income was a little over $25 a week. That small sum of money kept the wolf—but not the rats —away from our ghetto door. Working at such early ages taught us each the value of money, but it was a bleak existence. Being deprived of our childhoods, we all felt a sense of loss.

But as poor as we were, we always kept the traditional Jewish *pushke* (a small blue donation can) in our kitchen and when we could, we filled it with pennies and nickels in order to help Jews who were even poorer

18th and Carr circa 1930
MISSOURI HISTORY MUSEUM, ST. LOUIS

18th and Carr street. A Jewish butcher waits for customers.
MISSOURI HISTORY MUSEUM, ST. LOUIS

than us—although there was absolutely no doubt in my mind that we were the poorest Jewish family in the entire Carr Street ghetto.

In later life, after I had made millions in the business world, I liked to think that God had somehow smiled on me and remembered me and my family for putting those hard-earned pennies in that blue *pushke*. I believe that, in this world, an act of charity is never forgotten.

The Carr Street ghetto I grew up in was about seven square blocks in size and located on the north edge of downtown St. Louis. It abutted the now-razed Pruitt-Igoe public housing complex and the famous—or infamous—"Kerry Patch" neighborhood, which Irish immigrants began to settle in 1842. My ghetto was literally a United Nations: 40 percent

Jewish, 40 percent Italian, and 20 percent black. A few Irish also lived in our ghetto, and along with them came young toughs who belonged to dangerous Irish gangs always spoiling for a fight—gangs like Egan's Rats, the Hogan Gang, the Pillow Gang, the Red Hots, and the Cuckoos.

In many ways, the Carr Street ghetto resembled the massive lower East Side ghetto in New York City, which was the home of millions of persecuted and downtrodden immigrants who came to America at the turn of the century looking for the streets that were paved in gold.

The streets of my ghetto were filled with old and dingy tenements and junkyards. You saw aging Jews from the old country still wearing their traditional black clothes and *shtraymls* (black fur hats). Ancient women dried tomatoes in the sun. The streets also were home to peddlers' horses and wagons, hoodlums and hustlers all trying to make a buck any way they could. But the ghetto also housed hundreds and hundreds of honest, decent hard-working families who prayed to God that some day, somehow, they could flee this terrible affliction that was the ghetto and find a better life for their children and themselves.

When I was selling newspapers on freezing street corners, all I had to keep me warm was a fire I would build in a barrel. I had no winter clothes to speak of and the cold would penetrate my body to the point that I could barely rub my hands together to generate some warmth. And on such nights, I promised myself over and over again that one day I would live in a warm house, there would be plenty of food on the table, and I would never go hungry again.

And if it were not for the kindness of certain people, I could have starved. One Italian family, the Cantanzaros, was in the produce business and regularly gave our family fruit and vegetables to keep us going. A group of nuns gave me food, and the Salvation Army was a godsend. (To this very day, I regularly support the Salvation Army because I will never forget how they helped feed me.)

Typical storefront at 18th and Carr neighborhood
MISSOURI HISTORY MUSEUM, ST. LOUIS

The Corson family owned a grocery store and gave us credit when we didn't have a dime. And they never lost a penny with us. The Fixman family always paid their bills. And I will always have a special place in my heart in memory of Mark Kaufman. He owned a drugstore in the ghetto. I never had a few pennies extra to buy an ice cream cone, so Kaufman would permit me to lick out the insides of the ice cream containers after he was finished using them. What a *mitzva* (good deed) that was.

As a kid, I slept on a makeshift, narrow kind of cot (who could afford a bed?) nestled right next to a wall in our decaying flat. Slept is probably not the right word because every night I would lie quivering in fear, listening to a pack of rats gnawing away at the wall, just inches away from me. One night, my eldest sister, Celia, then about age 9, let out a scream of pure agony. A rat from the pack had gnawed through the wall, jumped onto Celia's face and had bitten her deeply right above her nose next to her eyes. The rat scuttled away after biting my sister, and we immediately rushed her to the neighborhood doctor, a Dr. Kohn. Celia nearly died from the massive infection that followed that rodent bite, but Dr. Kohn saved her life.

That's what it was like living in the ghetto. You had to not only fend off rats while you were trying to sleep, but you also had to fight Jew-hating gangs during the day while coping with constant hunger, never knowing where the next dollar was coming from for food. To survive the ghetto, it took the very *neshome* (soul) out of you.

Many young kids got in trouble in the ghetto. I mean big trouble. At least five youthful Italian friends of mine went to prison for robbery with long sentences that rubbed out their youth. Several young ghetto boys were convicted of murder. An offending pimp lost both of his legs when he was blown up in a car.

I learned from all of this and was very careful not to get into trouble with the law. But I also learned not to take any crap from anyone, no matter who it was. So one day in *cheder* (Hebrew School) when Rabbi Becker took a ruler and rapped me hard over my knuckles, I reacted immediately. I balled up my fist and slugged the Rabbi right in the middle of his beard. Of course, they kicked my 12-year-old ass right out of Hebrew School and that was the end of my formal Jewish education. When I got home and told my mother what I had done, I received the beating of my young life.

But being booted out of Hebrew School did not keep me from being *bar mitzvahed* (becoming a man in the Jewish tradition.) This was due to the efforts of Mr. Wexler, the junkyard owner, who was deeply educated in Judaism and who probably should have been a Rabbi.

When I was young, this building was the Hebrew Free School at 1727 Carr.
MISSOURI HISTORY MUSEUM, ST. LOUIS

When I was 13, Wexler took me to the *shul* on 15th and Wash Streets. He said, "Repeat after me," and then he let loose with a flood of Hebrew words that I tried my best to repeat back to him. That was it. That's how I was *bar mitzvahed*. It happened on a Thursday, not the traditional Saturday, and it was over in just a few minutes. I received no *gelt*, no watches nor any gifts, but it really didn't matter. I had become a man and I was extremely proud of myself.

When I went home, my mother told me to go to the grocery and get a 10-cent loaf of bread. On credit, of course. When I told the grocery owner, Mrs. Corson, that I had just been *bar mitzvahed*, she congratulated me. Then she punched the "No Sale" key on her cash register, opened the till and handed me 50 cents. I was dumbstruck. I felt like I was rich, but I went home and handed over the 50 cents to my mother because I was raised to be a responsible Jew who helped out his family. Was there any other way?

Although I had become a man in the Jewish tradition, I was still a 13-year-old kid hustling to help my family make ends meet. To supplement my income from my paper routes, I helped sell watermelons in the summer from a horse-drawn wagon on the ghetto streets. I made a meager 20-cents an hour, but every single penny was precious.

Every day in the ghetto was a dangerous one. In order to get to Carr School, my paper routes and back home again, I was forced to run three peril-filled gantlets and use my fists to survive fights with gangs that fought me bodily and tormented me mentally with their anti-Semitic slurs.

The first challenge was running four blocks from my flat to my grade

Carr School
St. Louis Public Library

Jefferson Hotel

school. Then, after school, I ran to my paper routes on various corners of downtown St. Louis: 12th and Franklin, 12th and Washington, at the Garrick Theater and the Jefferson Hotel, to name just a few. At night after selling my papers, I had to sprint home and fight off more toughs. My good friend, Jackie Dicker, the future pro fighter, would often run with me and we formed a two-man team fighting off the gangs. What a tough guy Jackie was! He was the kind of person you would want watching your back in a foxhole. He was what the Jews called a *schtarkeit*, a person filled with strength. The friendship we formed as kids in the ghetto lasted well over 70 years until Jackie was stricken with a fatal heart attack.

When I was 15 years old, I began to feel the stirrings of strong sexual urges. In other words, it was time to get laid.

My sexual rite of passage took place in a whorehouse located at Theresa and Lucas avenues. My two brothers-in-law took me there and then left the room to go about their own business. The door opened and in came a young prostitute who quickly quoted me the current prices as if she were reading from a short menu: 50 cents if you wanted a white woman; 25 cents if you preferred black.

I gave her 50 cents. She left and returned with a pot with soap and water and proceeded to wash me down. I got so excited that I climaxed in her washcloth. My "going off" before "going in" was a huge letdown, and I couldn't believe how quickly I had blown my precious money.

The next time I went back things were different. I took my sweet time and everything worked out just fine. However, along with rising erections, there came rising inflation. The whorehouse raised their price to $1 (I should only have had such huge markups when I was in business) but after all they were pushing one of the oldest commodities in the world, a product the public just could not live without. On my return visits, I chanced to run into several of the girls who had been my ex-paper route customers in the ghetto. And they remembered me. What a place for a reunion: smack in the middle of a bordello.

Even though I lived a miserable day-to-day life in the ghetto, I was smart enough to try and learn something helpful amid these squalid surroundings. As an example: There were 12 junkyards in the ghetto. I knew that number exactly because as a kid I poked and prowled around every one of them to make a few pennies here and there and to learn something about the worth of old batteries, scrap iron and other metals.

One scrap yard was owned by the Zeid family. Abe Zeid's wife, Bessie, did all the buying, selling and haggling over price, plus she handled all of the accounts (cash only, no checks, please). But while Bessie was busting her tail at the yard, Abe was out hunting for tail. Abe was the ghetto's Don Juan, an extremely handsome man who loved the ladies. Somehow, it all worked out and the Zeids did well with their business.

The Bakers were another unusual ghetto family. They owned a small grocery store, but it had no food. If you walked in and found two loaves of bread on a single shelf, you were lucky. The grocery was actually a front for all-day, all-night poker and gin rummy games. The Bakers were all outstanding gamblers, and that's how they made their money. Selling milk? Who needs it? Better to give the Bakers a pair of aces wired. They knew the correct odds in all the card games, an edge that made them consistent winners. So if you were a masochist, like most gamblers are,

The view looking up Delmar from 12th Street.
MISSOURI HISTORY MUSEUM, ST. LOUIS

you didn't have the edge and the grocery was the perfect spot to drop your hard-earned money. The store's motto should have been: "We're open night and day to take your cash away."

As you might expect, bootlegging was a big business in the ghetto. The king of the bootleggers was the head of the Scarfino family. Mr. Scarfino was "The Godfather of the Ghetto," a man feared by everybody. It was rumored that he held the power of life or death over people. If you chanced to meet him on the street, it was the right thing to respectfully say: "Good morning, Mr. Scarfino" and then quickly be about your business. No one in his right mind, no matter how tough you were or what gang you were in, would mess with or challenge Scarfino.

On Italian religious holidays, processions with statues depicting saints and other holy figures would pass through the ghetto streets, and on these occasions you would see Scarfino pinning dollar bills on the robes of the statues. Many decades later, when the *Godfather* movies captivated all of America, I would flash back in my mind to the ghetto and see Scarfino with his wad of dollar bills honoring the saints. He would have been a natural for the Hollywood role.

Another feared character in the ghetto was Mary Monkado, always known by her nickname of "Dago Mary." She was a bootlegger who dressed in black. Mary would always have a towel wrapped around her left arm and underneath that towel she toted a .45 caliber revolver. People were afraid of Mary and avoided her like the plague. Her husband was serving time for murder and her two sons, Jimmy and Sammy, were later gunned down in St. Louis.

If you were a ghetto kid, there was no money to buy an ice cream cone and a movie was absolutely out of the question. But we always found ways to amuse ourselves and pass the time. We told jokes to each other in Yiddish, listened to Yiddish music and made fun of each other by coming up with some creative nicknames. The nickname I liked best, of course, was my own, "Benny the Fix," but my next choice was Lou (Sugar) Adelstein. We called Lou "Sugar" because he was the sweetest, nicest guy in the ghetto. Some of the names we gave the other kids were unprintable.

Most of the time I walked around the ghetto without a penny in my pocket. If by chance, I had an extra 10 cents, I felt that I was on top of the world. I was always thinking of ways to make money when I struck up a friendship with a young man who worked for the *St. Louis Post-Dispatch*. He liked me and realized that I was as poor as a church-mouse. So he did me a great big favor. He gave me newspapers, which he took from the *Post-Dispatch* so I could sell them on my street corners and routes. It was all pure profit for me, and I never forgot him for his help.

SOME 40 YEARS LATER, AFTER I WAS SUCCESSFUL, I TRIED TO FIND THE YOUNG MAN FROM THE *POST-DISPATCH* BECAUSE I WANTED TO REPAY HIM FOR WHAT HE HAD DONE FOR ME. IN MY SEARCH, I ENLISTED THE AID OF A GOOD FRIEND OF MINE, DAVID LIPMAN, THEN THE MANAGING EDITOR OF THE *POST-DISPATCH*. WE NEVER DID FIND THE MAN, BUT THE WHOLE INCIDENT TAUGHT ME SOMETHING ABOUT MYSELF: NAMELY, THAT I WAS A LOYAL PERSON WHO WOULD MOVE HEAVEN AND EARTH TO HELP OUT SOMEONE WHO HAD BEFRIENDED ME, BUT I ALSO KNEW I HAD ANOTHER SIDE TO MY MAKEUP: IF SOMEONE FUCKED WITH ME, THEY HAD BETTER BEWARE BECAUSE I HAVE A LONG, LONG MEMORY.

MY MOTHER

There is a Yiddish expression: "*Siz nishto a schlecter mameh.*" The English translation is: "There is no bad mother."

Deep inside the hearts of the five Fixman children, we all felt nothing but love and respect for our mother, Rose, despite the scoldings and beatings we received when we got out of line. Our mother was always our Queen, our Rock of Gibraltar, a fearless woman with a spine of steel who did her best to raise her children against a backdrop of suffocating and grinding poverty.

Our mother controlled our lives—and that was a good thing because, without her, we would all have ended up in orphanages or have perished.

She would often tell us, "We may all starve, but we will starve together as a family." Her words and deeds sustained us and kept us alive. Without a word of complaint, she toiled as a cleaning lady, sometimes working for as little as 13 cents an hour to bring in some income.

She was so desperate and driven to find money that she even tried making bootleg wine in our bathtub. But it was a failed enterprise. She also tried making comforters stuffed with feathers but that didn't work out either. She had a grocery store at one time, a confectionery at another, but she was always undercapitalized. After all, how could you open a store with just $30 of capital? (I think the man who gave her the money was her lover. My mother was single at the time, but married twice after that. As my success in the business world grew, I supported all of her marriages.)

My mother, a strict Orthodox Jew, always saw to it that we lit the candles on Friday night and had a pre-Sabbath supper. Most of the time it was chicken because chicken was cheap, it tasted good, and chicken soup was supposed to be the panacea for anything that ailed you—from the sniffles to a raging fever.

My mother was a born improviser. When I needed new shoes—and there was no money to buy them—she took me to a surplus store and bought me some used tennis sneakers. When the soles got to the point that they were full of holes, I stuffed newspaper into the holes. That's how you survived in the ghetto.

Over and over again, my mother would tell me as a child, "*mein zindele, deigeh nisht,*" which meant, "don't worry, don't have a care." And then she would add in her broken English: "It will be all right. Someday you will grow up and be a businessman." She drilled those words into my head repeatedly. It was a refrain that never stopped. Later on in life, I realized that my mother had street smarts, and she somehow passed them on to me, her youngest son. Without them, I never could have made my mark in life.

I also respected my mother because she was a physically strong woman who could defend herself when trouble came along. One day she went to collect the back rent from a woman in our building. As she was demanding the money, the woman suddenly lunged at her with an ice pick. My mother wrested away the ice pick, and after that incident the rent money was always on time—and the landlord was happy.

One day, when I was 13 years old, my mother sat the family down and told us some truly wonderful news: We were moving out of the ghetto. I couldn't believe it, and neither could Celia, Nina, Martha and Hymie. I think we all cried, but they were joyous tears.

At that time, our family had just gotten off of relief. We were all working steadily and bringing in a little more money. That money made our exodus from the ghetto possible.

So in 1938, the Fixman family relocated five miles west to 1384 Clara Avenue, a West End neighborhood that was predominantly Jewish, a neighborhood that was much nicer than where we had come from.

What a difference five miles can make. We were now living in a neighborhood where I was still hustling newspapers, but it was a place where you could walk the streets at midnight and still feel safe. Rarely was anyone attacked, but if a woman were accosted, her attacker would wind up in a sewer—compliments of several Italian men who policed the neighborhood and saw to it that people acted properly and abided by the law. It was a kind of vigilante justice.

I was now enrolled in a new school, Emerson Grade School. Naturally, as the new kid on the block, I had to prove myself with my fists. But these were not gang battles; they were exhibitions between kids to see who was the best "duker." That's where my ghetto experience as a fighter kicked in. I won every one I fought. Not a single loss in the bunch. Pretty soon the challenges all faded away.

On Clara Avenue, we had trees and yards and a real sense of safety. The neighborhood was made up mostly of duplexes and a few four-family flats.

My reputation as a fighter soared when I beat the living shit out of a kid named Eddie Cola, a neighborhood tough guy with a big reputation as a duker. Eddie tried to pick my pocket one day and I made short work of him. When kids heard that I had cleaned Eddie's clock, they never gave me any trouble. None at all.

At Emerson School, I always wanted to dress nicely to impress my classmates, especially the girls, who were just starting to bloom. But there was always the problem of money. Money went to pay the rent. New clothes? Out of the question.

Once again, my mother came to the rescue. She got a neighbor to lend her $10. She then took me to Safron's Department Store in Wellston and bought me a navy blue suit. I was so proud that I didn't take it off for eight months. I wore it every single day to school. At night, I would press the suit, putting a wet cloth over it and steaming

Emerson Grade School

In my new neighborhood, I was introduced to the
original Jewish Community Center at 3636 Page Ave.
MISSOURI HISTORY MUSEUM, ST. LOUIS

it so I could keep the trouser creases as sharp as the edge of a knife. But the kids at school, kids who came to class every day in different outfits, were no dummies. They soon figured out that the navy suit was my only outfit, and I took a lot of ribbing from them. But I didn't care because I owned that navy suit.

After Emerson, I was a freshman at Soldan High School on Union Boulevard. Attending Soldan was a bittersweet proposition. I really enjoyed the classes and my teachers, but there was a downside, too. I hated to go to school every day wearing the same old clothes, while my classmates wore many different outfits. But the worst was sitting in the school cafeteria and watching everyone having lunch. I skipped lunch most of the time because lunches cost money and I didn't have any. It made me feel like an outsider with a big chip on my shoulder.

Soldan High School
MISSOURI HISTORY MUSEUM, ST. LOUIS

After just eight months at Soldan, I was forced to drop out to help support my mother and the rest of the Fixman family. At this time, my brother, Hymie, was in Koch Hospital suffering from tuberculosis. He was in the hospital for three years.

That time at Soldan was the extent of my formal education—just eight months of high school. As I walked down the steps of Soldan for the very last time, tears streamed down my face. CU

CHAPTER TWO

I ENTER THE BUSINESS WORLD AS A JANITOR

At age 15, I entered the business world as a janitor. I couldn't know it at the time, of course, but it was the beginning of a success story that could only have happened in America.

I was damn glad to get the janitor's job at Worth's, an eight-store, five-department women's ready-to-wear chain. Actually, my sister Martha, who worked at Worth's as a saleslady, heard about the opening and got the job for me.

The job paid $10 a week—big bucks at that time for a 15-year-old ex-ghetto kid. On my very first day working in a Worth's warehouse in thriving Wellston, I made a promise to myself: I would work my ass off at my new job. I wanted to learn all facets of the business, because I certainly didn't want to push a broom forever. (You should see Wellston today; it looks like an A-bomb landed on it.)

Alvin Goldfarb, who ran the entire Worth's operation, was impressed with the fact that I was working 60- and 70-hour weeks. Alvin took me under his wing and also taught me how to drive his 1939 Pontiac, which I later used to deliver merchandise to the stores.

Alvin was my mentor and I idolized him. One day he took me aside and said, "Benny, you've got what it takes. You are a workhorse." That compliment left me floating in the air, and I was even more determined to succeed at Worth's. At the end of three months, Alvin raised my salary to $12 a week; after six months, I was making $14 weekly, and

The Wellston Terminal was one of the major transfer points in St. Louis, circa 1947. The City of Wellston was one of the busiest shopping areas in St. Louis from 1930s until late 1950s when I worked at Worth's.

HTTP://FREEPAGES.HISTORY.ROOTSWEB.ANCESTRY.COM/~HAEFNER/

at the end of a year, I was bringing home $17.50 a week. All the while, I was offered more management-type responsibilities. By 1943 when I was 18, Alvin had bumped me up to the princely sum of $32 a week.

It's funny but nearly 70 years after having worked for Worth's, I can still remember the inventory code: 0024 was for Bally girdles, 0025 was for Hollywood Vette Bras, and so on. (Today, at the age of 84, I carry more than 100 telephone numbers in my head. Rolodexes? Who needs them?)

One day in the warehouse, a German man named Schildnick befriended me. He knew that I was an uneducated Jewish boy and he wanted to help me out by impressing on me the value of having a large

THE DICTIONARY HABIT BECAME INGRAINED WITHIN ME AND WHEN I BECAME A BUSINESSMAN, I ALWAYS HAD ONE HANDY BECAUSE I HAD AN ONGOING ZEST FOR KNOWLEDGE. ALTHOUGH I HAD BEEN FORCED TO DROP OUT OF HIGH SCHOOL, I WAS STILL SMART ENOUGH TO REALIZE THAT YOU NEEDED KNOWLEDGE AS A PATHWAY TO POWER IN THE BUSINESS WORLD.

vocabulary. Schildnick, who worked for Monarch Marking Systems that manufactured marking tags, began teaching me words. The first word he laid on me was "circumvent," which, of course, drew a blank, but not for long. I immediately bought a dictionary and I began to look up every new word Schildnick challenged me with.

In 1943, with World War II raging, I decided to volunteer and go into the U.S. Army. There were horror stories coming out of Europe about millions of Jews dying in Nazi concentration camps and I wanted nothing more than to get into the fight and kill some Germans.

When I told my mother that I was volunteering, she showed great concern and worry that something terrible might happen to me. She wasn't at all happy about her youngest son becoming a soldier, but my mind was definitely made up.

The next thing I knew, my buddy, Leo Cosentino, and I were both inducted into the Army at Jefferson Barracks in St. Louis. I was only stationed at Jefferson Barracks for a few days, but that was long enough for me to lose my life-savings of $200 in a crooked game of craps. The *ganefs* (crooks) who busted me out were a smart bunch of hustlers who rigged the game by "cackling" the dice so that they could throw certain points. I should have known to be more careful, but a few months later my street smarts helped me to get my lost bankroll back—and much more.

I got orders detaching me from Jefferson Barracks to recruit training duty at an Army base in Palacios, Texas. Palacios was a tiny town located about halfway between Houston and Corpus Christi. The Palacios army base was definitely not the place for a nice Jewish boy who had to share his sleeping hut with five other soldiers, all *goyim* (Gentiles) of course. But at least there were no ghetto rats to deal with, just a few rattlesnakes now and then.

Now I was ready to make back my lost bankroll of $200. I made friends with the guys who had cackled the dice at Jefferson Barracks, and now I was on their side, the winning side. I soon had my bankroll back, plus I was making a killing at the poker games that sprang up in camp. I was excellent at playing poker. I never chased the cards (that was for idiots), and I knew all the percentages. I would wait patiently for a strong hand to come along, and then I would bury those other mothers. It was like a license for minting money.

But I faced a physical problem that was burying me: *pes planus*, that's Latin for flat feet. When the Army forced the recruits to make 15- and 20-mile marches with a full pack, I couldn't keep up. My flat feet left me in agony. There was absolutely no way I could negotiate a long training march.

While all of this was going on, I was thinking about my mother and the rest of the Fixman family. I was on the phone to her constantly. Of the $50 the Army paid me every month, $30.95 was sent home to her and I got to keep $19.05 for myself, which was more than adequate since I was getting three square meals a day and I was killing the suckers at poker.

I made a real pest of myself in the Army. I bitched constantly because I was so very worried about how my mother was doing. My growing

reputation as a *kvetcher* (complainer) coupled with my aching flat feet—
the Army doctor said he had never seen a worse case of *pes planus*—
combined to get me out of the Army after serving 4¹/₂ months. I received
an Honorable Discharge "at the convenience of the Government."

Some of the other kids I had grown up with were far less fortunate.
Isadore Pultman was killed in the Battle of Normandy, and Ely Eagle lost
his life later on in the battle for Europe.

Many of my childhood friends ended up in the ill-fated 555th Coast
Artillery Battalion Anti-Aircraft Unit, which was involved in the war's
bloodiest and most crucial battle, the Battle of the Bulge. Ill-fated is the
precise term to describe their fate because the 555th sustained a 50 percent
mortality rate.

After my short hitch in the Army, I went back to work for Alvin
Goldfarb at Worth's. He welcomed me back like a lost son, as the father
I never knew.

In my late teens, I was already a well-known figure at two of St. Louis'
most famous ballrooms and pick-up spots, Tune Town and Casa Loma.

Casa Loma Ballroom

Dressed in a semi-zoot suit attire, complete with a prominent key chain, I would samba, rumba, jitterbug and ballroom dance my way across the floor. I always had an eye out for a possible conquest. It was make-out city. The girls who flocked to Tune Town and Casa Loma knew why they were there: They were all looking for action.

On my nights on the prowl, I never used my real name when meeting chicks. Instead, I adopted the names of two Italian men who lived miles away in downtown St. Louis. In one ballroom, I was known as Ben Apollo; in the other, my moniker was Ben Menaci. The rationale behind all of this deception was simple: I found out as a man-about-town that it was much easier to get laid being Italian than being Jewish. Why? I'll never really know. Maybe it had something to do with anti-Semitism. But I do know that Messrs. Apollo and Menaci scored repeatedly.

What I could not know at that time was that my nights at Tune Town and Casa Loma were about to come to an abrupt end because of a four-letter word: love.

YMHA (Young Men's Hebrew Association) building on Union Blvd.
MISSOURI HISTORY MUSEUM, ST. LOUIS

I MEET THE LOVE OF MY LIFE

One fine summer day in 1944, I walked into the Worth's store near the Fox Theater—and my life changed forever.

It was truly love at first sight—and the name of this beautiful young redhead was Marilyn Schneider.

I found out that Marilyn was working Saturdays part-time while attending high school. I was so taken by her beauty that I couldn't get her out of my mind. Even at age 15, Marilyn was breathtaking, dazzling—absolutely stunning.

One night I chanced to be hanging out at the YMHA on Union Boulevard. There was a beauty contest being held at the "Y" and, of course, Marilyn was the winner. When I saw her being honored, my feelings for her only deepened.

After Marilyn walked off the stage, I grabbed her and pushed her into a telephone booth in the lobby and started kissing her. People were walking past the phone booth and watching us carrying on. But their presence didn't stop me one bit. I had never experienced feelings like this in my young lifetime. I was 19 and Marilyn was just 15. (She laid a little story on me, claiming she was 17, but I knew better.)

I didn't care what age she was. I only knew one thing—that this was the young woman I wanted to spend the rest of my life with. Marilyn and I began dating and we quickly fell in love with each other. But there were problems: Her parents, Abe and Rose Schneider, did not like me one bit.

They both thought that I was a young, rough-and-tumble hoodlum who should never be dating their daughter. In truth, I was an extremely hardworking young man who wanted desperately to succeed in life.

But Abe and Rose would not change their minds about me. In fact, they were so upset over our relationship that they shipped Marilyn off to Kansas City so she would be far away from me. But in my heart, I knew nothing could keep us apart because our love was *bashert* (destined to be).

I was so certain that Marilyn would return to me that I slept in my car at night in front of the home of Marilyn's aunt, Eva Corn. Eva, who liked me and knew of my deep affection for Marilyn, roused me from my sleep one night and told me to get out of my car and come into her home for something to eat—an act of kindness I still remember to this day.

Sure enough, Marilyn returned from Kansas City the very next day and we were closer than ever.

Every Saturday night, I would take Marilyn dining and dancing at the "in" spot in St. Louis, Harold Koplar's Chase Hotel. On one of those lovely evenings together at The Chase, following a two-year courtship, I asked Marilyn to marry me. I knew she would say yes. But when she did, it was truly the happiest moment of my young life.

The Chase Park Plaza Hotel
MISSOURI HISTORY MUSEUM, ST. LOUIS

When her parents heard of our engagement, Abe, a shoemaker who knew how tough it was to grind out a living every day, confronted me and said: "How are you going to take care of my daughter? How are you going to provide for her and the family you will have?"

I told him, "Don't worry. Marilyn will be well provided for. I promise you I will take care of her for the rest of her life." And I did exactly that. I kept my word.

Shortly after that, Marilyn and I were married at the DeSoto Hotel in downtown St. Louis. We spent a week's honeymoon at the Drake Hotel in Chicago. It was a joy-filled week that I will always remember except for one bad incident.

Illustration of the DeSoto Hotel, in downtown St. Louis

The Drake Hotel, Chicago

One night, I took Marilyn to the Chez Paree, Chicago's most famous night/supper club. We were having dinner when three tough looking men and a woman sat down next to our table. Almost immediately, the air was filled with profanity of the worst kind and the men started playing with the woman right at the table. I was brokenhearted that my bride had to endure the profanity and the sexual advances. And I was mad as hell. I got up from our table and went over to theirs. I asked them to stop the cursing and the fondling of their woman companion. From their looks, I quickly figured out that they were Chicago racketeers with mob connections. One of the three men told me to shove off. I felt my blood boil and I wanted to take them on even though it was three against one. But I decided to hold my peace and not ruin the evening. So I went back to my table and Marilyn and I finished dinner.

When we exited the Chez Paree, the three men followed Marilyn and me out of the supper club into the street. When I saw them approaching, I knew there was going to be a fight. I was trying to figure out which one of the three I was going to hit first. The odds didn't bother me because when I lived in the ghetto, I was often outnumbered and I always managed to survive. Suddenly, one of the men extended his hand and said: "We're sorry about the profanity. We were out of line." With the apology came an offer to pick up our tab. I accepted the man's apology, but I wouldn't be his guest. Why? Because when you put yourself in the position of accepting a favor from those kind of people, they always want something in return. So I said to him: "Thanks, but no thanks."

Chez Paree, Chicago

An even more unsettling event occurred upon my return from my honeymoon. Alvin Goldfarb, my boss at Worth's, reneged on his promise of a $1,500 bonus. He told me I would only get $500. When Alvin cut my bonus, I cut my ties with him and Worth's. I remember what my mother always drummed into me: "Your word is your bond. Always keep your word and never, never trust people who break their word with you."

When I told Alvin I was leaving, he was shocked. He tried to win me back by raising my weekly salary from $165 to $200, figuring that would do the trick. But I was a ballsy young man and I told him to forget about it.

I was now 22 years old and jobless, and although I didn't know it at the time, Marilyn was pregnant. Since I had saved up a little nest egg of $3,000, I considered going into the ladies' ready-to-wear business on my own. But I knew from my experience at Worth's that $3,000 was a pittance as far as obtaining a really prime sales location. So I decided that business was not for me.

When I look back, that decision was a major turning point in my life. The only other business that I knew about was the scrap metals business and that's where I put my nest egg. I started out small but by the time I was finished, I had revolutionized the U.S. scrap metals industry and forged a business empire. CU

CHAPTER THREE

TIME TO HIT THE ROAD

In 1947, I took $1,500 from my precious nest egg and purchased a new two-ton Dodge truck. I borrowed $500 from my father-in-law for working capital. With these two assets, the truck and the money, I entered the scrap metals business.

In my new enterprise, I made money from day one. I was a *kokhlefl* (a go-getter) in business because I was now a family man and there were mouths to feed.

My truck proudly bore the name: MJB Metals. M for my wife Marilyn; J for my infant daughter Janis; and B for Ben, owner and driver.

At first, I worked the states of Missouri and Illinois, calling on gas stations and mechanics' garages and buying their discarded batteries and scrap iron. I quickly branched out into three other states: Kentucky, Iowa and Indiana.

I bought such a large volume of batteries that in just a few short months, I became known in the trade as "The Battery King of the Midwest." I usually paid $1.50 for a discarded battery and I made between 25 cents and 50 cents in profit when I resold the battery to wholesale metal dealers. That may not sound like a lot of profit, but because of the thousands of batteries I was buying in five states, that business was a solid profit center.

My purchases of batteries and scrap metals were all done on a cash basis. I kept my bankroll in my shoes. When I made a deal, I would go into the men's restroom, take out the cash from my shoes, and then pay the man what I owed him. In those days, cash was truly king. People really didn't like doing business using checks because they knew that occasionally one would bounce higher than the proverbial kite.

1947 Dodge truck

When I got to a small town, I would immediately check out the scrap yards and the people who owned them. I would say that 90 percent of the yard owners were Jewish, and nearly all of them spoke Yiddish. Being able to converse in Yiddish with these fellow Jews was an instant icebreaker that enabled me to land their business. After all, why do business with a *goy* (a Gentile) when you could do business with one of your own kind?

It seemed that many of the scrap dealers I did business with had unmarried daughters who were desperate to change their station in life, hoping to find a nice Jewish man to settle down with. Accordingly, I received many invitations "to come to my home for dinner and meet my beautiful daughter." When I told them that I was already a happily married man, the disappointment quickly registered on their faces.

One dealer in Mt. Vernon, Ill. said to me: "So you're married. That's all right. You could have two wives: one in St. Louis and one in Mt. Vernon." Then he added: "I'm only joking." But I wasn't too certain that he was.

Working on the road 15-16 hours a day was a certified ball buster because of all the lifting and loading of heavy metals that was involved.

But most of all, it was dangerous. When your truck carried 30,000 pounds of batteries, iron scrap, auto parts, crankshafts and camshafts, there was the ever-present danger of the entire load shifting on you and crushing you to death. But someone must have been looking out for me, because I never had so much as a fender bender in all my years of driving. And I was on the road constantly, often driving 2,000 miles or more in a week's time.

I ran my business on a strict schedule and knew my costs down to the penny. (I even amazed my CPA, Marvin Blum, with the way I handled numbers.) A typical week for me would run like this: I would leave our apartment and hit the road on Monday, along with one helper. I would buy as much scrap material and batteries that I could and return to St. Louis late Tuesday night. On Wednesday, I would sell my materials in St. Louis to various dealers. On Thursday, I was back on the road again for another round of buying, lifting and loading. On Friday night, I would return to St. Louis and on Saturday I would sell my materials again. Come rain, snow or high water, I never deviated from this schedule.

Generally, on Saturday nights, I would take my wife and infant daughter out to dinner. We would first stop at the best barbecue restaurant in St. Louis, Vic's Barbecue. (It was rumored that Vic's secret sauce that made the meat taste so good was really the sweat that ran down Vic's arms while he was preparing the food.) Sweat or no sweat, it beat all the other barbecue joints in St. Louis—and the prices were great for my pocketbook. After Vic's, the next stop was "Sam the Watermelon Man," acknowledged to have the best watermelons west of the Mississippi River. And that would be our evening.

We were a happy Jewish family. Marilyn and I were deeply in love and our infant daughter, Janis, was a God-given addition to our household.

But what a rough start tiny Janis had in life. Because we were so low on money, I was forced to rent in northwest St. Louis. We had a bedroom but had to share the bathroom with a family named Murphy. The rent was $10 a month. Marilyn and I shared that one bedroom and our infant daughter had to sleep in the top drawer of a dresser before I was able to afford our own apartment and purchase a crib for her.

And one day we nearly lost our 6-month-old baby. I was asleep on our couch in the late afternoon when I heard Marilyn scream: "Ben, get up. The apartment is on fire." Then she screamed even louder: "Get Janis. Get Janis." By now our apartment was filled with thick, choking smoke. I jumped up, told Marilyn to run down the stairs to safety and bolted into our bedroom to get Janis. The smoke was everywhere. I grabbed Janis from her crib, got down on my knees and using my free hand, propelled myself across the floor until I was free of the bedroom. I raced down the stairs and into the street with Janis in my arms.

By now the firemen had arrived. Both Marilyn and Janis were unharmed, but I was coughing my guts out. Then it hit me: I had left my bankroll of $3,000—all the money I had in the world—on top of the dresser in our bedroom. A fireman ran with me as I went to save my bankroll. But he had on a gas mask and I didn't. Back into the smoking apartment I went. I managed to recover the $3,000 but in doing so I was hit by a second barrage of choking smoke. When I reached the streets for the second time, I was in bad shape and was breathing convulsively. They took me to a hospital, treated me for smoke inhalation and kept me overnight before releasing me the next day. Police said some kids were fooling around with matches and that was the cause of the fire. But I didn't care about who set the fire; all I knew was that I had saved the life of my infant daughter, and I gave thanks to God for being able to do that.

But even as my scrap business prospered, the economic climate in the country was changing ominously. In 1949, a nationwide recession occurred, burying tens of thousands of businesses, including mine.

I was forced to shut down because I was no longer able to find markets for what scrap I could buy. But in my travels on the road, I had gotten my feet wet in the industry and witnessed a lot of wasteful practices that should have and could have been eliminated in order to improve a company's bottom line. In short, I had gained valuable insight for the future—and I put this insight to good use when the right time came.

Having been forced to close my business, I was now in deep financial trouble but I was not about to let it get me down. I was too much of a fighter for that to happen.

So after the recession struck, I went into the landscaping business and I was doing well for myself when out of the blue a home building strike took place, which forced me out of business again. It was like a double whammy. First, a national recession, and then the building strike. Now my nest egg shrunk even further and I spent some worrisome nights thinking of how I could support my family.

So I hit the streets again, selling Baby Tendas (protective baby chairs) on credit to young mothers in poor neighborhoods. The chairs were not cheap—they cost $49.95—but I sold them like hotcakes. One day, I set a company-wide record by selling 30 Baby Tendas, going door-to-door.

I also supplemented my income from the baby chair business by running a once-a-week poker game from my apartment. I did very well in this dollar-limit game because I always played under control unlike the floppers who wanted to play every single hand, a sure recipe for losing all your money.

But selling baby chairs and running poker games were only temporary measures to keep me afloat. I was literally aching to get back into the scrap metals business. When

Baby Tendas

prices began to stabilize in late 1949, I jumped right back in—going on the road again but with a bigger goal in mind: targeting manufacturing companies that produced high volumes of industrial materials.

In looking for such companies, one day I made a cold call on Airtex Products of Fairfield, Illinois, a well-established re-manufacturer of fuel pumps.

I met with Airtex's general manager, Henri Barre, an affable Frenchman who told me to go out into the factory and find a Mr. Jackson, who would give me some material samples. Then Barre told me to come back in two weeks or so and give him my price list.

I found Mr. Jackson and got the samples. But as far as waiting two weeks to come back to Airtex with my price list, that was simply out of the question. What was I—some kind of *meshuga* (a crazy person) who would wait two weeks while a competitor sneaked in and stole the business from me? Not by a long shot. So the very next day at 6:30 a.m. and after I had gotten my samples, I camped right on the front steps of Airtex waiting for Mr. Barre to come to work. The price list he had requested was right in my hand.

> WALKING INTO AIRTEX WAS LIKE STROLLING INTO A LAS VEGAS CASINO AND MAKING 12 STRAIGHT PASSES AT THE CRAP TABLE. IN SHORT, AIRTEX PROVED TO BE A GOLD MINE.

Barre was deeply impressed that I had given immediate attention to the matter and had not waited the two weeks he had granted me. But he was even more impressed with my prices because he was about to save millions of dollars on a long-range basis.

For instance, Airtex was selling a load of scrap material to a dealer from Mt. Vernon, Ill. For that load, Airtex received $50 from the dealer. For the same load, my offer to Airtex was $3,000 (on which I still made a healthy profit). Barre couldn't believe his eyes. He scanned the rest of my price list, liked what he saw, and then he said to me: "Ben, you've got our business." It was an account I served for more than 10 years.

In all, Airtex had three plants employing some 2,000 workers. Not only did I make them millions on scrap transactions, I also helped them realize enormous savings by modernizing their production processes.

Airtex was disassembling the pumps manually, a truly wasteful method. I told Barre that manually taking apart the pumps bordered on insanity. What he must do is install a sweat furnace to bring about greater efficiencies in the production cycle. Barre followed my advice, installed the sweat furnace and profitability soared at Airtex.

By now, I had developed such a positive rapport with Barre and Airtex that I became known around their plants as "the Jewish boy who walked on water." I could do no wrong.

One day Barre sat me down in his office and said: "How do you know so much about metals and manufacturing? I know you are only 24 years old. Where did you learn all of this? Do you have a degree in metallurgy or in engineering?"

I told him the truth: I was a high school dropout who relied on "Jewish engineering" to solve problems.

Barre said he never heard that term before. What is it? It's simple, I told him: With Jewish engineering you either solve the problem or you starve to death.

Besides landing Airtex, I was now able to establish business relationships with several other companies that produced large volumes of scrap metals. These included Dowser Electric and General Radiator, both situated in Mt. Vernon, and Central Iron and Metals, located in Springfield, Ill.

My industrial scrap business was booming and I was still the "The Battery King of the Midwest." But by now I had my fill of working the road. I wanted to be back in St. Louis, closer to my growing family and my loving wife, Marilyn. And I also wanted to buy my own scrap yard.

The yard I wanted was located at 2219 Delmar Blvd., just seven blocks from where I was born 26 years earlier, right next to Willy Wexler's junkyard on Carr Street.

I wanted that scrap yard badly, but I didn't have the $22,000 the owner was asking.

So I turned to my old friend, Willy Wexler, for help. Wexler said, "absolutely no problem" when I told him I wanted to borrow $22,000. "Benny," he said, "I have known you since you were a kid. Your word was good then and it's good now. I know you are good for the money."

Wexler gave me the $22,000 without any loan papers being signed, without me having to put up any collateral, and the loan was to be interest-free. It was all done on a handshake. That's how friends did business in those days.

Try walking into a bank in today's world and asking for a $22,000 loan, without any interest, without any collateral, and without any papers having to be signed. Here's what would have happened: The loan officer would call for a bank guard and you would be tossed out into the street before you could blink an eye.

Needless to say, I repaid the $22,000 loan in full within a year. I now had a formal base of business in St. Louis—a scrap yard of my very own. The year was 1951.

The moral of this story is: "Never break your word because your entire reputation is at stake. In life, your word is your most important asset."

But I was impatient to grow and owning just one scrap yard was not enough for me. So in 1954, Irv Fischer—one of the sweetest, most gentlemanly persons to ever grace the scrap industry—and I formed Fischer-Fixman Metals Co., a non-ferrous metals wholesaler located

first at 3000 Clark Avenue and then relocated to 4239 Duncan Avenue
in mid-town St. Louis.

Duncan Avenue location

NOT TOO LONG BEFORE I WAS ABLE TO PERFECT THE
COLD PROCESS, A DISASTROUS ELECTRICAL FIRE SWEPT OUR
DUNCAN AVENUE PLANT. I FELT AS IF MY LIFE HAD COME
TO AN END BECAUSE THE FIRE PUT US OUT OF COMMISSION
FOR APPROXIMATELY 60 DAYS AND BURNED UP OUR
EQUIPMENT AND INVENTORY.

BUT THAT FIRE ONLY SERVED TO DELAY—BUT NOT PREVENT—
THE COLD PROCESS FROM COMING TO FRUITION. THAT'S WHAT
HAPPENS WHEN YOU HAVE PERSEVERANCE ON YOUR SIDE.

But Irv and I had totally different business dispositions. I was so obsessed with revolutionizing the staid American scrap industry that I almost drove Irv crazy.

Clearly, it was time to split. So I bought Irv out in two stages. I gave him $60,000 and 10 percent of the stock in the first stage, and then two years later, in 1956, I paid Irv another $60,000 for his stock. I kept the same company name until 1962, when it was renamed Diversified Metals Corp. CU

> IRV FISCHER AND I REMAINED LOYAL FRIENDS FOR DECADES. WHEN HE ASKED ME TO TAKE HIS TWO SONS, KENNY AND ELLIS, INTO MY BUSINESS, I DIDN'T HESITATE FOR A SECOND. AND I GAVE BOTH OF THEM IMPORTANT JOBS WITH MY COMPANY.

The trucking fleet of Diversified Metals Corp. covered the country.

CHAPTER FOUR

"THE SCRAPPER FROM ST. LOUIS"

(that's what *The New York Times* called me)
**"revolutionizes metals reclamation in America
with the development of the Cold Process."**

Most people wake up at night for a trip to the john, but one night I bolted out of bed at 1 a.m. because during my sleep I had finally solved a vexing technical problem that would totally change the face of metals reclamation in this nation and would make Diversified Metals a future star on Wall Street.

I shouted at my wife, Marilyn: "I've got it. I've got it. I've finally found the solution." She replied: "Are you crazy?" Then she rolled over and went back to sleep.

I immediately called Leo Paradoski, my executive vice-president, and told him, "Leo, meet me at the plant right away. I'm pretty sure I've solved the problem."

For well over 50 years, the metals industry had been trying to figure out how to separate copper and aluminum wire from its insulation without using heat—traditionally dumping the material in a field and putting a match to it or else using incinerators. Both methods were inefficient and created dangerous pollution.

When Leo and I met at the plant, we quickly proved that my solution —called the Cold Process—was workable. We were able to mechanically separate the steel from the copper and aluminum and other elements like various grades of plastic.

The Cold Process rendered heating methods passé. When perfected, it produced pure copper and aluminum pellets called Nuggets, which turned out to be perfect for use in the chemical plating and foundry industries. The process also eliminated the highly toxic gases produced in the heating method. Among them were phosgene gas (a lung irritant), sulphur, hydrogen chloride and carbon monoxide.

Diversified had spent two years and expended more than $250,000 in trying to find an alternative to the burning method. Frankly, as a then small company, we were just about busted out and nearly at the end of our rope when I woke up that night in 1961 and cried: "I've got it."

Once again, Jewish engineering—solve the problem or starve to death—had prevailed. But our days of nearly starving were over. Thanks to the Cold Process, we went on to earn $5 million in one year alone.

The Cold Process was the turbocharger responsible for our meteoric rise. In 1961, our sales were just below $4 million; by 1967, they had risen to nearly $100 million.

The mechanical process we had developed greatly helped to curtail air pollution and made Diversified one of the very first green companies in the United States. Everyone jumped on the green bandwagon as years went by, but truth be told, we were a leading pioneer in making our air better to breathe.

When word got around in the industry that Diversified was now using the Cold Process for reclamation, people started to beat down our doors. In short order, we were doing business with some of the biggest corporations in the country: AT&T, Essex Wire and Cable, General Cable, Anaconda and Phelps Dodge.

For many years, companies with much larger assets than Diversified had tried to find a reclamation process that didn't rely on burning. But all their efforts had failed despite the fact that their engineers were from some of the finest schools in the country, schools like M.I.T., Cal Tech and Georgia Tech.

But these engineers—despite their degrees up the yin-yang—couldn't

The Dismantling Division of Diversified Metals performed
projects of all sizes on a nationwide basis.

Diversified's copper nuggets. They revolutionized the industry.

unlock the secret and find the Holy Grail. To my way of thinking, they missed the boat because they did not have the right combination of *saichel* (brains), common sense, street smarts and creative imagination. Many of them were what I termed "degreed idiots and educated fuck-ups." Many of them lived in their own ivory towers, completely oblivious to what was happening in the real world outside.

So in the end, it took a Mad Jew (myself) and a brilliant Pole (Leo) to come up with the Cold Process and beat all those smart engineers to the finish line.

Naturally, we tried to protect ourselves by patenting the Cold Process, but the lawyers said it was not patentable because it was similar to other types of technology.

My advisers then told me not to worry because it would take the competition years and years and years to come up with a comparable non-heat technology.

Wrong.

In just two years, other firms had copied our process, thanks in part to a campaign of industrial spying that put Diversified squarely in their sights. So once again, my trusted advisers—with all their college degrees and a false sense of superiority—had given me some bad advice. So more and more I began to rely on my own gut feelings when making business decisions.

But being the first to come up with the Cold Process did have its rewards. Soon we were operating four "pollution-proof" plants nationwide, in St. Louis and on the East and West Coasts. Business was booming. And in 1965, I built a 300,000 square foot plant in North St. Louis County and our days on Duncan Avenue—where it all started—were over.

In March of 1966, I took Diversified Metals Corporation public and personally cashed in $9.5 million for myself, which was actually like putting perfume on a hog. I thought to myself: "With that kind of money, I could have bought the entire neighborhood where I grew up as a paper boy, where I used to buy a 10-cent loaf of bread on credit, where I was a man before I was a boy."

Diversified's stock offering was a smashing success on Wall Street. The stock came out at $9 a share and climbed to $132, creating millionaires among the people who worked for me and who had earned stock options that were dirt-cheap.

With DMC stock the toast of Wall Street, I began to receive calls every single day from analysts looking for information. In the classic

When Diversified went on the New York Stock Exchange, Lawrence Powers (right) and I were greeted by a NYSE official. Powers, a Wall Street lawyer, provided me with legal advice over the years.

movie, *Wall Street,* actor Michael Douglas utters the immortal line that "Greed is good." And most of the stock analysts I spoke with lived by that creed. What a bunch of con artists they were. I mostly toyed with them, played things low-key and hard to get and let them help my stock to rise. But I never gave them the inside information that they craved although they were a tenacious bunch of moochers.

Besides bringing in millions in business, the perfection of the Cold Process created a wave of positive publicity throughout the industry. As an example, in 1969, *Scrap Age,* the recognized bible of the metals industry, named me as its "Man of the Century." (See plate 2)

What they wrote was so full of praise that it was a little embarrassing. Here are a few excerpts from the *Scrap Age* article: "In truth, few people in the metals industry have had so meteoric a rise to fame and fortune as Ben Fixman has.

"Ben is an alley-wise street fighter who was definitely NOT 'born to the purple,' having been born in a ghetto in St. Louis.

"Ben is little changed by his success. He is still regarded as just 'one of the boys' by his friends, and if you are a friend, his loyalty knows no bounds. But if anyone tried to cross him in a business deal, it turns out that Ben has a long memory. His greatest pleasure is still making a profitable business deal, and after making one, he will shout for the whole office to hear: 'I love it.'"

A *New York Times* article called me: "The Scrapper from St. Louis." The larger headline for the story read: "A New Horatio Alger Tale." The story stated: "I had a chip on my shoulder. I had to prove to myself that I was as good as the people who had an opportunity to get a formal education. I was driven. I also had the advantage of being one of the younger men in the scrap business. Most young men don't want to go into the scrap metal business today, and that was true twenty years ago, too. I could see opportunities that my competitors couldn't."

I told *The New York Times* reporter that because of economic conditions we started acquiring companies to protect ourselves against disintegrating economic conditions. By this time, we had changed our name to Diversified Industries and we eventually acquired 36 separate companies producing everything from ballpoint pens to fabrics. We were a Fortune 500 company from 1969 through 1972. In 1971, we reached our high mark in sales volume—more than $330 million." (See list of Diversified's subsidiaries on the next two pages.)

But this turned out to be the wrong road to travel. We should have stayed specifically in the metals field, without going so far afield, I told the reporter, adding that, "from now on, our emphasis is going to be on growth in the metals area. In metals processing technology, we are just at the beginning."

The Times story closed by calling me "a philanthropist who refuses to discuss his philanthropies ... a man who generously rewards those who are productive and loyal ... a man who never forgets or forgives a double-cross."

The Associated Press, Business Week and *Forbes* magazine all printed glowing articles about the Horatio Alger theme of my life and the company's Cold Process. How did that make me feel? Honestly, pretty damn good. After all, what human being doesn't like to receive a little praise now and then? I looked at it this way: It couldn't hurt and it could only help.

I particularly liked *The Associated Press* story by reporter Mike Recht. It started off by saying: "Ben Fixman is sitting on top of a scrap pile, but he has made it so comfortable, he may never come down.

"Fixman, by developing the Cold Process, has taken the smoke, dirt and grime out of the junk business and made it a pollution-free, lucrative operation for his company."

I told *The Associated Press* the truth when I said: "I feel good

Diversified Industries' Subsidiaries

COMPANY	PRODUCT	HOME OFFICE
American Home Products	Sporting Goods Departments	Providence, R.I.
Avita Health & Fitness Products, Inc.	Exercise Equipment	Seattle, WA
Boxer Department Stores	Department Stores	Columbia, MO
Consolidated Unit, Inc.	Automobile Replacement Parts	Newark, N.J.
Consumer Home Products, Inc.	Housewares and Hardware Departments	St. Louis, MO
Cuyahoga Wrecking Corp.	Dismantling-Wrecking Structures	Cleveland, OH
Datatron Processing, Inc.	Computerized Mailing Service	Nassau, NY
Diversified Dismantling Corp.	Dismantling Telephone Cable & Wire	St. Louis, MO
Diversified Metals Corp.	Nonferrous Metals Processing	St. Louis, MO
Diversified Metals International, Corp.	International Metals Trading	New York, NY
Diversified Insurance Agency, Inc.	Insurance Agency	St. Louis, MO
Drachman Structurals, Inc.	Warehousing and Distributor of Structural Steel	New York, NY
Duro Pen Corp.	Pen Manufacturing	Long Island, NY
Eastern Diversified Metals, Corp.	Wire & Cable-Nonferrous Metals Processing	Tamaqua, PA
Fox Industries, Inc.	Warehousing	Madison, IL
George Sall Metals, Inc.	Ingot Maker & Smelting of Aluminum	Philadelphia, PA
Insurance Programmers, Inc.	Insurance Agency	St. Louis, MO
Kemco Metal Products, Inc.	Nonferrous Metals Processing	St. Louis, MO
Kimco Auto Products, Inc.	Automobile Replacement Parts	Memphis, TN
Kolker Insurance Agency, Inc.	Insurance Agency	St. Louis, MO
Liberty Smelting Works, Ltd.	Nonferrous Metals Processing	St. Jerome, Can.
M&R Plastics and Coatings, Inc.	Plastic Product Manufacturing	St. Louis, MO
Metal Supply Service, Inc.	Nonferrous Metals Processing	Hammond, IN
Middlewest Freightways, Inc.	ICC Common Carrier	St. Louis, MO
N.S. Colen & Sons, Inc.	Nonferrous Metals Processing	Los Angeles, CA

North American Development Corp.	Building Demolition	New York, N.Y.
Pioneer Synthetics, Inc.	Synthetic Bag Manufacturing	Kansas City, MO
Plume & Atwood Brass Mill	Brass Strip Manufacturing	Thomaston, CT
SM&R Co., Inc.	Jewelry and Photo Departments	Chicago, IL
Scullin Steel, Co.	Manufacture Railcar Components	St. Louis, MO
Synthetic Industries, Inc.	Manufacture Synthetic Carpet Backing	Chickamagua, GA
Theodore Sall, Inc.	Nonferrous Metals Processing	Philadelphia, PA
United Refining & Smelting Co.	Precious Metals Refining	Franklin Park, IL
Western Diversified Metals, Corp.	Nonferrous Metals Processing	Cucamonga, CA
AVA Steel Products, Inc.	Wire Rod, Merchant Shapes	St. Louis, MO New York, NY
AVA-Toshin Service & Supply Corp.	Japanese Manufacturing Technology	Tokyo, Japan St. Louis, MO, New York, N.Y.

■ ■ ■

Junkman To Captain Of Industry

By Gerald J. Meyer
Of the Post-Dispatch Staff

BEN FIXMAN, born in the fabled old Kerry Patch area near downtown St. Louis, is the founder, chairman and guiding spirit of Diversified Industries, Inc., listed by Fortune Magazine this year as the 337th largest industrial corporation in the United States.

He is a world traveler, a subject of conversation in high places, a close acquaintance of at least one chief of state — Prime Minister Golda Meir of Israel.

And as one of Fixman's lieutenants said recently, "That ain't bad for a junkman." It also ain't bad for a man who started working when he was 6 years old, dropped out of high school in his freshman year, and 30 years ago was selling baby beds from door to door.

It would not be bad, in fact, for one of Horatio Alger's sterling Victorian heroes. But Fixman is one of a kind. If St. Louis doesn't know much about him, it's only because Fixman himself prefers to keep things that way.

He has all the requirements to become a living legend except one. He doesn't want to be famous.

The non-legend of Ben Fixman began, naturally enough, when he was born here 45 years ago. It took its first Algeresque turn a year and a half later, when his father died. His mother, an immigrant who couldn't speak English, was left with five young children.

*Close friends asked me if I was offended when
the St. Louis Post-Dispatch called me a "junkman." "Absolutely not,"
I replied. "That's how I made my fortune."*

JUNKMAN TO CAPTAIN OF INDUSTRY
BY GERALD J. MEYER

BEN FIXMAN, BORN IN THE FABLED OLD KERRY PATCH AREA NEAR DOWNTOWN ST. LOUIS, IS THE FOUNDER, CHAIRMAN AND GUIDING SPIRIT OF DIVERSIFIED INDUSTRIES, INC., LISTED BY FORTUNE MAGAZINE THIS YEAR AS THE 337TH LARGEST INDUSTRIAL CORPORATION IN THE UNITED STATES.

HE IS A WORLD TRAVELER, A SUBJECT OF CONVERSATION IN HIGH PLACES, A CLOSE ACQUAINTANCE OF AT LEAST ONE CHIEF OF STATE—PRIME MINISTER GOLDA MEIR OF ISRAEL.

AND AS ONE OF FIXMAN'S LIEUTENANTS SAID, "THAT AIN'T BAD FOR A JUNKMAN." IT ALSO AIN'T BAD FOR A MAN WHO STARTED WORKING WHEN HE WAS 7 YEARS OLD, DROPPING OUT OF HIGH SCHOOL IN HIS FRESHMAN YEAR, AND 20 YEARS AGO WAS SELLING BABY BEDS DOOR TO DOOR.

IT WOULD NOT BE BAD, IN FACT, FOR ONE OF HORATIO ALGER'S STERLING VICTORIAN HEROES. BUT FIXMAN IS ONE OF A KIND. IF ST. LOUIS DOESN'T KNOW MUCH ABOUT HIM, IT'S ONLY BECAUSE FIXMAN HIMSELF PREFERS TO KEEP THINGS THAT WAY.

HE HAS ALL THE REQUIREMENTS TO BECOME A LIVING LEGEND EXCEPT ONE. HE DOESN'T WANT TO BE FAMOUS.

THE NON-LEGEND OF BEN FIXMAN BEGAN, NATURALLY ENOUGH, WHEN HE WAS BORN HERE 45 YEARS AGO. IT TOOK ITS FIRST ALGERESQUE TURN A YEAR AND A HALF LATER, WHEN HIS FATHER DIED. HIS MOTHER, AN IMMIGRANT WHO COULDN'T SPEAK ENGLISH, WAS LEFT WITH FIVE YOUNG CHILDREN.

Partial text from the Post-Dispatch *article, 1970*

about finding a pollution-free process, but I did it only for the money. Why lie? Life's too short."

As our business grew, I noticed a disconcerting trend in America: People just didn't want to work. Things got so bad that we couldn't find enough people to properly operate our new 300,000 square foot plant in North St. Louis County. Even a special bus service right to our front door from the inner city didn't do the trick.

I got so aggravated that I ran huge display ads in both of St. Louis' major newspapers, the *Globe-Democrat* and the *Post-Dispatch*, in which I vented my feelings.

The headline read: "Diversified Metals Tells It Like It is …We give a Damn." The advertising copy read:

"Frankly, we're tired of hearing people constantly complaining that they can't find a job or if they do have one, there's little chance of advancement, or that the 'world is against them' and they must live forever in a poverty area waiting for the mailman with their next welfare check.

"Laziness and indifference never helped one bit in building this great America, and if those attitudes aren't checked they could very well destroy the greatest nation on earth.

"We at Diversified Metals have worked long and hard to build one of America's major metal companies. As a result of our labors, our business has never been better, but frankly despite our untiring efforts, we have been unable to find people to fill the many jobs that have gone begging the past few months.

"So, we are appealing directly to you—the unemployed. So if you want to work and work hard, step forward and be counted. WE NEED YOU. WE GIVE A DAMN."

The next day, we hired 36 people. The day after that, 27 of them quit. Diversified Metals proved to be the launching pad for many

Recovered chrome pressed into bars

As the old ad says: Diversified Metals Corp. —"The only one of its kind."

executives who eventually left and started their own metals operations. To a man, each one was highly successful and it gave me great pleasure to see them succeed and to know that Diversified was such a perfect training ground. Look how the world has changed. In today's economy, do you think there would have been any quitters? Not one in a carload.

In looking back, the decade of the 1960s represented a spectacular span of achievement for Diversified.

In 1967, I made two colossal, multi-million-dollar moves in the copper market—moves that would have seemed impossible for an ex-ghetto kid to have come up with and execute to perfection.

The beauty of both these moves was that there was absolutely no risk to Diversified or its shareholders. There was no downside, only a highly profitable upside.

In the first move, Diversified bought and owned ALL of the copper on the London Metal Exchange (LME). The total amount of copper purchased was some 13,000 tons, worth millions and millions of dollars.

We bought all of the LME contracts because I had found a ready-made buyer for all of that copper. The buyer, one of the nation's largest manufacturers of wire, was so pleased with the prudent and protective manner in which I handled the deal that they let me have every one of their production plants in the United States and Canada for the handling of their huge amounts of by-products.

In the second deal, Diversified purchased ALL of the copper on the New York Commodity Exchange (COMEX). This was another riskless deal because I had already pre-sold the COMEX copper—and the tonnage was huge—to one of the world's largest industrial companies.

My peers in the industry knew that I had a reputation for never revealing industrial secrets, and because I played my cards "close to the vest," this helped to seal both copper deals. Bragging was for idiots. I just kept my mouth closed and counted the cash.

Eventually, my life-long belief that college degrees don't mean diddly-squat in achieving success in the business world was confirmed in a story written by David Brooks, the highly acclaimed and richly talented columnist for *The New York Times*' op-ed page.

His column (May 19, 2009) quoted a study reporting that the traits that correlated most powerfully with business success were attention to detail, persistence, efficiency, the ability to analyze situations and the willingness to work brutally long hours.

My interpretation of the Brooks column was that you can take all the MBA degrees in the world and "put them where the sun doesn't shine." Degrees, to my way of thinking, are just pretty pieces of paper that don't guarantee you even one bit of success in business. It's what INSIDE of a person—that's the important factor in business and in life. CU

CHAPTER FIVE

I LOSE THE TRUE LOVE OF MY LIFE

I believe that every man—if God or good fortune shines upon him—will find the one great love of his lifetime. This is the story of how I lost the only woman I ever truly loved.

One night in our bedroom, Marilyn said she had to talk to me. "Honey," she said, "there's something wrong with me. I've been to the doctors and taken a bunch of tests. They say everything is O.K., but I know better because I can feel a lump in my breast."

Within days, Marilyn, who was 36 years old at the time, underwent surgery at Jewish Hospital in St. Louis. Her surgeon was her first cousin, Dr. Sam Schneider.

After what seemed like an eternity, Sam came out of the operating room with tears streaming down his face. "Ben, I removed a cancerous growth from Marilyn, but her cancer is aggressive and advanced. At best, she has 90 days to two years to live."

When I heard that death sentence pronounced, I came apart mentally. I went into a state of shock and panic and began bawling like a baby. But I kept repeating to myself: "I must keep Marilyn alive. I must keep Marilyn alive. I must keep the love of my life and the mother of our three daughters alive."

I didn't know where to turn until I remembered that my business partner in Chicago, Harold Brady, had once attended medical school before he went into the scrap business.

My favorite photo of Marilyn

I called Harold immediately, told him of Marilyn's dire prognosis and he replied: "The cancer expert you should contact is Dr. Irving Ariel at the Memorial Sloan Kettering Cancer Center in New York." (Irving Ariel later left Sloan Kettering because he did not think they were aggressive enough in their approach to treating cancer.)

Irving Ariel was to become Marilyn's main doctor and was instrumental in overseeing the treatments that prolonged her life. We became very close friends and he once confided in me: "If you fight a wild animal [cancer], what do you do? You grab anything you can and strike back at it."

Most doctors follow traditional paths in treating cancer—going by the book as they say. Not Irving. He developed a reputation as an innovator, a doctor who was willing to try new methods. And because of his success with these new methods, he quickly acquired a reputation as one of the top cancer experts in the nation. When he came to St. Louis to treat Marilyn, the entire St. Louis medical community acted as if God himself had descended upon them.

I was certainly glad to have a man with such credentials on my side. In his 14-plus years of treating Marilyn, Irving never sent me one bill for his services. But in return, I helped him financially in publishing more than 240 medical journal papers dealing with cancer treatment, plus the seminal 12-volume work he wrote with Dr. George T. Pack, *The Treatment of Cancer and Allied Diseases.*

After Irving examined Marilyn, he decided her best chance for survival was to insert radioactive isotopes into her mammary glands. This was a revolutionary procedure that was many years before its time back then in the mid-60s, but Irving was not a slave to medical precedent—and my own gut-feeling was that I had found exactly the right surgeon to treat Marilyn.

Irving inserted the radioactive isotopes into Marilyn in an operation performed at Doctor's Hospital in New York. At first, the doctors didn't want to let me into the room because of the threat of radiation. But they relented when I told them there was no chance of my becoming impotent since I had a vasectomy when I was 35 years old.

The radioactive isotope therapy seemed to help Marilyn somewhat, but even as a layman, I could tell she wasn't coming along as well as I wanted her to.

In fact, she started to regress and I told that to my dear friend, movie star and comedian Red Buttons. A well-known German doctor named Dr. Hans Nieper had successfully treated Red's wife, Alicia, for throat cancer. This was the same doctor who also successfully treated actor Fred MacMurray when he came down with throat cancer.

Red told me: "Ben, you better take Marilyn to Germany to see Dr. Nieper. You know he saved my wife's life and Fred MacMurray's, too. I think it's certainly worth a shot."

The next thing I knew Marilyn, now in a wheelchair, and I were in Hanover, Germany, consulting with Dr. Nieper. He prescribed a combination of experimental treatments heavy on vitamins and diet.

We stayed in Hanover for two weeks until Marilyn was finished with her treatments. Marilyn no longer needed her wheelchair and was able to eat some decent food for the first time in months. We were both elated.

But cancer is a tenacious and insidious disease. Over the next few years as Marilyn's condition gradually worsened, I took her to see cancer experts at hospitals in Houston and Miami. I refused to give up, but the best medical minds in the country were unable to arrest her spreading cancer.

The chemotherapy she was receiving had terrible side effects. She was in constant, unremitting pain and finally she was put on morphine to ease her agony.

Our three daughters, Janis, Barbara and Jody, and I were grief-stricken to our very roots as we helplessly watched Marilyn diminish. We wanted to help her so very much, but she was beyond our help and all we could do (besides trying to comfort her and cheer her up) was to cry our eyes out.

By now, I had put a hospital bed next to my bed in our bedroom. I had nurses for Marilyn around-the-clock. They took excellent care of her; they all admired her for her dauntless spirit, which never wavered during her ordeal.

Every minute of every day, I thought of my Marilyn. I thought of what a wonderful wife and mother she was. I thought of her loving feelings for every member of our entire family. I thought of the many kindnesses she had extended to people throughout her life. I thought of the honesty and humility she displayed in all her dealings with other people. I thought of the fact that she had never changed—or become carried away with herself—from the very first day I chanced to meet her when she was just 15—a gorgeous, red-haired, breathtaking beauty.

And I thought that if there was one single word to describe Marilyn, that word had to be majestic. For Marilyn was truly the most majestic woman that I had ever known.

During her final days, Marilyn said she had something she wanted to discuss with me.

"Honey," she said, "I have $400,000. I wouldn't have that money unless you gave it to me. I'm going to leave that money to you. I want you to do two things for me: See that my mother, Rose, is taken care of for the rest of her days and see that my sister Thelma's children all are educated." (Thelma was actually not in need of help since her husband left ample insurance money when he died of a brain tumor.)

I said: "Baby, do you want me to draft up a document regarding your mother?" "No," she answered. "I know you are a man of your word and will take care of Rose." And I did until the day Rose died.

Very shortly after that, Marilyn passed away. I held her in my arms in our bedroom as tears rolled down our cheeks. The day was November 4, 1980; Marilyn was 52 years old.

It was the darkest day of my life. It sent me into a deep depression.

In Marilyn's memory, I founded the Marilyn Fixman Cancer Center at Jewish Hospital in St. Louis, which I still support to this day and which has helped thousands of people afflicted with cancer.

Marilyn's favorite flower was a yellow rose. So I inaugurated a "Yellow Rose Ball Party" at the Chase Hotel in her memory. And I matched every dollar of contributions.

On the wall in my office hangs a large, gallery-size portrait of Marilyn dressed in a beautiful gown. (See plate 1) I look at that picture every day and I still cry. In truth, a majestic person like Marilyn only comes this way once in a lifetime. CU

After Marilyn passed away, I founded—in her memory— the Marilyn Fixman Cancer Center at Jewish Hospital in St. Louis.

CHAPTER SIX

I BACK A BIG BROADWAY SHOW
BUT A CRITIC'S BLAST COSTS ME MY ASS

In the winter of 1980, shortly after my wife Marilyn died, two friends, well-known theatrical producers Don Gregory and Mike Merrick, approached me to invest in a new musical ultimately targeted for Broadway.

The show was called "Copperfield" and was, of course, based on the novel *David Copperfield*, written by one of the world's most famous authors, Charles Dickens.

I became more interested in getting involved when Gregory and Merrick said they would invest their own money in the show. To me that was proof that they both believed "Copperfield" had a chance to become a smash hit on "The Great White Way."

The credentials of the multiple-award winning Gregory and Merrick were impeccable. They worked together to produce "My Fair Lady" and "Camelot." Merrick conceived "Clarence Darrow" starring Henry Fonda, and "The Belle of Amherst" with Julie Harris, which won a Tony.

But I knew nothing about the novel itself. So I had a little research done for me and the results of that research were as follows: "Many of the world's greatest writers and thinkers revered the book. Among them was Sigmund Freud, who said *David Copperfield* was his favorite novel. While being held captive in a Soviet prison camp, Fyodor Dostoyevsky read it and was enthralled. Leo Tolstoy said Dickens was the greatest of all the English novelists and considered the book his favorite novel. The book was also heavily praised by Henry James, Franz Kafka, James Joyce and Virginia Woolf."

Due to my lack of a formal education, the names Joyce, James, Kafka and Dostoyevsky didn't ring a bell with me. For all I knew, these people might have been linebackers in the National Football League.

I had another reason for investing: When I saw the title "Copperfield," I thought of the word the title contained: copper. Copper had always been lucky for me ever since I left that ghetto so many decades ago.

I had made my fortune trading copper, which enabled me to support my family. I always wore a thick-linked copper bracelet around my wrist—just for good luck—and in my home were works of art produced by "The Art of Nuggetry," in which the main ingredient were copper Nuggets manufactured by the company I had founded, Diversified Metals.

I was so fascinated and enamored of copper that I had the illustrator of this book draw in a few strands of copper-colored hair for the front cover. I never had a speck of red hair in my life—my hair was always jet-black—but a little copper couldn't hurt. If it's possible to have a love affair with a specific metal, I did exactly that.

Another reason I was attracted to investing in the play was that David Copperfield's life story and mine were very much alike. As the *Post-Dispatch* reported in an interview that ran before the play opened in St. Louis, Gregory termed the novel by Dickens "a prototypical rags-to-riches success story of the waif who never wavers. It is a story of optimism." When I read Gregory's words, I thought that's the same kind of optimism that kept me alive through my ghetto years and my breakout into the world of business.

Gregory added: "Coming from nothing, making your own way,

respect for your elders. My eyes fill up every time I watch a run-through of this show. I am supposed to be the hard old producer, and as I am watching this story unfold, I keep pinching myself."

Gregory went on to praise the music in "Copperfield," saying it's the most melodic score we've heard in years and the sets are just spectacular.

When I read Gregory's comments, I became even more excited over the show's prospects and I kicked myself mentally for not having taken a bigger part of the action as an investor.

But when Red Buttons heard that I was about to become a "Broadway Angel" by investing big bucks in "Copperfield," he went ballistic. "Benny," Red said, "you are an absolute maven in copper but you don't know dick about the theater. The chances of taking "Copperfield" and turning it into a big hit are the proverbial SLIM and NONE. You would get a better return on your money by opening a K-Mart in Jerusalem that only sold crucifixes to Orthodox Jews."

Another good friend of mine, New York businessman Harry Silverman, who knew the theater business inside and out, also warned me about investing in "Copperfield." "Ben, it's just like going to the crap tables in Vegas," Silverman said. "If you go there, the chances are good that they will nail you."

Harry was a man I really respected. Earlier I had invested $50,000 as a part of a large group seeking control of 20th Century Fox. Harry had brought me in on the venture, promising me that if I lost my $50,000, he would guarantee that he would send me back my money. "Harry," I told him, "I'm a big boy. If I blow the 50 grand, that's the way it goes. I'm not looking for any guarantees in life." Well, the attempt to control 20th Century Fox failed, and my money was lost. Or so I thought. Months later, I received a letter from Harry containing a check for $50,000. It's nice to deal with people who live by their word.

OPENING NIGHT—AND A GREAT REVIEW

My expectations soared even higher after the play opened (March 3, 1981 at the American Theatre in downtown St. Louis) and I read the rave review written by critic Judy J. Newmark of the *Post-Dispatch* (see page 86).

She called "Copperfield" a "joy to behold" and added: "In terms of sheer visual beauty, of luscious costumes, and awesomely invented sets, this musical may be in a class by itself—or at least a class that's been pretty empty since the lavish days of Florenz Ziegfeld."

The critic had high praise for the "Fair Scene," which integrated "all of the play's visual elements so beautifully that it looks like a gigantic valentine, or fireworks in pastel."

For two weeks the musical played to packed audiences who loved it. One night, during an intermission, Frank Pierson, general manager of the American, grabbed me by the lapels and said: "Benny, it looks like you've got yourself a big winner. The next thing is to take it right to Broadway." Naturally, I was elated that a man like Pierson, who had been around the theater for endless years, thought so highly about "Copperfield."

So off "Copperfield" went to the Big Stage: Broadway.

It opened at the ANTA Theater on 52nd Street, west of Broadway. New Yorkers also loved it and the theater was full for every performance. This went on for some 30 days, but "Copperfield's" success came to a screaming halt after a highly critical review by *The New York Times* critic Frank Rich. In a review published April 17, 1981, Rich blasted "Copperfield." He called it a "clunky, often incoherently told melodrama." He said "Copperfield might be entertaining for young children, whose innocent minds aren't sullied by memories of superior shows that this one dimly recalls." That review was the kiss of death for "Copperfield."

Ticket sales immediately dried up as big-ticket brokers quickly shunned the show. The audiences grew smaller and smaller every night. I had heard through the grapevine that Rich was going to pummel the show, and my information was correct. (My *mazel* [luck]—Rich joined *The New York Times* in 1980 as chief drama critic. Couldn't he have stayed wherever he was for a couple of years longer so he would not have had the opportunity to rap the show?)

Exactly nine days after the review by Rich, another *New York Times* critic, Walter Kerr, laced into the show with a second negative review. Kerr said the play "looks like a musical, but the actors can't make it act like one."

I thought to myself: "Why in the world would any paper print two highly critical reviews of the same musical?" If it were football, the refs would have called a "piling on" penalty.

Finally, there was only one thing left to do and that was to pull the plug on "Copperfield." Audiences in St. Louis and New York adored it but the critics didn't go for it and that was the end of the story. I had always heard about "the power of the press" and now I had seen a vivid demonstration of that power.

If "Copperfield" had been a success, I would have given a significant share of the profits to the fight against cancer, which took Marilyn's life, and which is an endeavor I still support financially.

In the end, I took my losses from "Copperfield" like a big boy, but I made a pledge that I would never again invest in any play or movie as long as I live. It's just like investing in the stock market; it's another person's game, and when you play, you will end up on the wrong side of the ledger.

An afterthought: Charles Dickens is buried in the "Poet's Corner" of Westminster Abbey, which is England's so-called "Coronation Church" and final resting place for 17 English monarchs. What they could really use at Westminster Abbey is an "Investors Corner" for a *meshugener* (a crazy man like me) and other "angel investors" who thought they could beat the odds and come up with a smash show on Broadway. Believe me, it's a tough road to hoe.

(FROM THE *ST. LOUIS POST- DISPATCH* 3/6/1981)

"COPPERFIELD" DEBUTS AT AMERICAN

BY JUDY J. NEWMARK

OF THE POST-DISPATCH STAFF

MOST OF THE TIME THE OLD EXPRESSION, YOU NEVER SAW ANYTHING LIKE IT, IS NOTHING BUT AN EMPTY PHRASE. HOWEVER, IN THE CASE OF "COPPERFIELD," THE MUSICAL THAT HAD ITS WORLD PREMIERE THURSDAY NIGHT AT THE AMERICAN THEATRE, IT IS LITERALLY, STAGGERINGLY, GORGEOUSLY TRUE. IN TERMS OF SHEER VISUAL BEAUTY, OF LUSCIOUS COSTUMES AND AWESOMELY INVENTIVE SETS, "COPPERFIELD" MAY BE IN A CLASS BY ITSELF OR AT LEAST A CLASS THAT'S BEEN PRETTY EMPTY SINCE THE LAVISH DAYS OF FLORENZ ZIEGFELD.

OH, THE PLAY'S PRETTY GOOD TOO.

NATURALLY IT IS NOT A GREAT DEAL LIKE THE CHARLES DICKENS NOVEL, *DAVID COPPERFIELD*, ON WHICH AL KASHA AND JOEL HIRSCHHORN HAVE BASED IT. THE BOOK WHICH HAS AN EXTREMELY COMPLICATED PLOT THAT OBVIOUSLY COULD NOT BE COMPACTED INTO A MUSICAL TRACES THE EMOTIONAL GROWTH OF A TROUBLED, ARTISTIC YOUNG MAN, WHO WONDERS WHETHER OR NOT HE WILL PROVE TO BE THE HERO OF HIS OWN LIFE.

In the play, all he gets to be is its centerpiece. The focus is shifted away from Copperfield (who is played as a child by Evan Richards and as an adult by Brian Matthews, in both cases with the requisite good looks and gallantry), and to the wonderful array of eccentrics who surround him.

It's a smart decision, one that director/choreographer Rob Iscove has utilized to create a lively theater of character sketches. There is Mary Stout's warm, rosey Peggotty, the kindly nurse who seems prepared to look after David until he's senile; Carmen Mathews' brisk Aunt Betsey, another of David's unlikely protectors, tossing her bonnet and gloved hands with imperial authority; George S. Irving's florid Mr. Micawber, always at a loss for money but never for words or true generosity. And best of all, there is Barrie Ingham's spidery Uriah Heep, spinning a sticky web of greed coated with false humility.

When these characters are on stage which, given their numbers, means practically all the time the play is delicious. Ingham and Irving each have a strong musical number, too. *Umble*, Ingham's leitmotif, features a vigorous dance in which, among other things, he lies on the floor murmuring thank you as Matthews dances across his back. And Irving's optimistic *Up the Ladder* is the one that you're likely to find yourself whistling.

IN GENERAL, HOWEVER, THE SCORE IS WEAK, ESPECIALLY IN SLOW, EMOTIONAL SONGS THAT ARE ALL TOO REMINISCENT OF OTHER MUSICALS (PARTICULARLY, IF UNSURPRISINGLY, *OLIVER!* AND LACK REAL FLAVOR OF THEIR OWN. THIS MAY BE BECAUSE, IN ORDER TO TRANSFORM *DAVID COPPERFIELD* INTO A MUSICAL, SO MUCH OF THE BOOK'S DISTINCTIVE TONE HAD TO BE MELLOWED DOWN TO A SIMPLER, LESS MOODY PITCH.

BUT THIS IS NOT A SHOW TO LISTEN TO, IT'S ONE TO LOOK AT. TONY STRAIGES' SET, FULL OF MOBILE AND DETAILED PIECES RANGING FROM FACTORIES TO CAROUSELS, IS PERFECTLY ACCENTED BY KEN BILLINGTON'S LIGHTING. IT IS EXTREMELY HANDY THAT "COPPERFIELD" TAKES PLACE IN THE EARLY 19TH CENTURY, A TIME OF RAPID CHANGES IN FASHION, SO THAT COSTUMER JOHN DAVID RIDGE WAS ABLE NOT ONLY TO DESIGN LOTS OF BEAUTIFUL CLOTHES, BUT TO DESIGN THEM IN DIFFERENT STYLES. IF LADY DIANA IS LUCKY, SHE WILL FIND A WEDDING DRESS HALF AS CHARMING AS THE ONE LOVELY MARY MASTRANTONIO GETS TO WEAR HERE. THE FAIR SCENE INTEGRATES ALL THESE VISUAL ELEMENTS SO BEAUTIFULLY THAT IT LOOKS LIKE A GIGANTIC VALENTINE, OR FIREWORKS IN PASTEL.

"COPPERFIELD" IS A BREATHTAKING REMINDER THAT THE ASPECTS OF THEATER FREQUENTLY DESCRIBED AS TECHNICAL ARE A RICH, INTENSELY CREATIVE, LIVELY ART. IT IS A JOY TO BEHOLD.

IT RUNS THROUGH MARCH 15 AT THE THEATER, NINTH AND ST. CHARLES STREETS, WITH 8 O'CLOCK EVENING PERFORMANCES (7 P.M. ON SUNDAYS) AND MATINEES AT 2 O'CLOCK ON SATURDAYS AND SUNDAYS.

■ ■ ■

As I look back on my life, I realize that show business people and celebrities always attracted and intrigued me.

One of my favorites was my friend, George Jessel, whom I was first introduced to in the 1960s at the Hillcrest Country Club in Los Angeles.

The Bronx-born Jessel was truly a piece of work, a man who was a revered entertainment star in multiple endeavors.

Known as "The Toastmaster General of the United States," Jessel achieved fame as an actor, singer, songwriter and Academy Award-winning movie producer, and for his frequent role as the master of ceremonies at political and entertainment gatherings in the United States and Israel.

George started acting when he was 10. He appeared in vaudeville acts on Broadway stages in order to help support his family after his father's death (a strange parallel to my own life story.)

The next year, he partnered with Eddie Cantor in a kid sketch. They performed together until George outgrew the role five years later. In 1925, he got his big break on Broadway when he landed the starring role in the stage production of "The Jazz Singer."

In the mid-1940s, Jessel started producing musicals for 20th Century Fox. In all, he produced 24 films for Fox in a career that lasted three decades.

Jessel also loved the ladies. His affairs with such stars as

George Jessel

Pola Negri, Helen Morgan and Lupe Valdez were all well known to the general public.

One day I heard that Jessel was in terrible financial trouble. I visited him in his humble apartment in Los Angeles and wrote him a check for $3,000. "When do you want me to repay this money?" Jessel asked me. I told him to forget about it. It wasn't necessary. Shortly thereafter, I was about to write Jessel a larger check but he suffered a fatal heart attack. I still miss George to this day. It was just great to be around him.

But Jessel was not the only world-famous star that I met at the Hillcrest Country Club. The other was Edward G. Robinson, known widely for his "tough guy" roles in the movies. It turned out that Robinson and I both spoke perfect Yiddish, and in no time at all, we became friends and began to amuse each other with stories and anecdotes—all spoken, of course in Yiddish. CU

CHAPTER SEVEN
DAVID (BENNY) VERSUS GOLIATH

After many years as a businessman, I developed the infallible Fixman Formula regarding how business cycles affect companies: "Good, Good, Good, then Bad."

The translation: Business runs profitably for years and years. Then, out of nowhere, a killer black cloud appears to destroy all that you have busted your ass to build.

In our case, the black cloud that came out of the blue was AT&T, the largest non-industrial corporation in the world. For years and years, AT&T regularly supplied 65 percent of all the plastic insulated wire that was processed at our four pollution-proof plants in St. Louis, Canada, California and Pennsylvania.

Then without one single word of their intentions, AT&T, which had spied on our operations, cut off their supply of materials to all of our plants and went into the business themselves in furtherance of a grand scheme of monopolizing the market.

When AT&T closed the spigot on Diversified, it was like a karate chop to our vitals. In 1977 and 1978, we had to shut down three of our processing plants.

There were only two ways to take the loss of our biggest customer: (1) accept it meekly and go on with our business or (2) fight back vigorously. Naturally, I selected option No. 2.

I decided to go right to the top of AT&T's management. That was

MY ASSESSMENT OF AT&T WAS DEAD ON. IT WAS A CLOSED-DOOR GENTILE CORPORATE COUNTRY CLUB THAT BELIEVED IT COULD DO ANYTHING IT WANTED AND THE PUBLIC BE DAMNED. IT WAS EXTREMELY HARD TO FIND A JEWISH PERSON AMONG THE AT&T MANAGEMENT TEAM. IN 1970, DEBUTTS— KNOWING DIVESTITURE OF THE BELL COMPANIES WAS INEVITABLE— RETIRED EARLY, ENDING HIS REIGN OF ARROGANCE FOREVER. IN 1973, AT&T HAD ENTERED INTO A CONSENT DEGREE WITH THE U.S. EQUAL EMPLOYMENT OPPORTUNITY COMMISSION, AGREEING TO HIRE MORE WOMEN AND UNDERREPRESENTED MINORITIES.

John deButts, the chairman who oversaw this monster company with its $70 billion in revenues. I knew that deButts had surrounded himself with a swollen layer of executive vice presidents, senior vice presidents and just plain vice presidents. So if I sent him my proposal via a letter, he would most assuredly "pass me off" to one of those vice president types and I would end up spinning my wheels in vain and accomplishing nothing.

Therefore, a face-to-face meeting with deButts was absolutely essential in advancing my strategy of trying to win back the AT&T business.

I knew that John deButts was an extremely difficult man to get a sit-down with, but I had an ace in the hole. That gentleman was St. Louisan Sidney Salomon, who was an extremely politically connected and highly successful insurance agency owner. Salomon also owned the St. Louis Blues Hockey team and, at one time, was a part owner in the old St. Louis Browns American League baseball team. I later found out that Salomon had some strong leverage over deButts because of several tremendous favors he had done for the AT&T chairman.

Sid and I were close friends, and so when I asked him if he had the right connections to set up a meeting with deButts, he replied: "Ben, no problem. I'll get back to you in a few days."

Sure enough, Sid got back to me almost immediately and said deButts had agreed to see me at AT&T headquarters in New York City. Sid accompanied me to the meeting with deButts and several high AT&T executives.

Call it paranoia, or call it whatever you want, but the very instant I walked into deButt's office, I felt as if I was back in the old ghetto of my childhood, facing off once again against a bunch of anti-Semites.

The meeting lasted one hour, and I went through my whole shtick in telling deButts that if AT&T would remain a Diversified customer and not go into the business themselves, I would save AT&T $20 million in guaranteed profits. I also offered to sell deButts our four strategically located processing plants which would have saved AT&T millions of dollars in freight costs annually. (He didn't know it, but I was actually an expert on AT&T and its operations. Through information I had gained over the years, I probably knew about as much about AT&T as deButts did—maybe more.)

DeButts listened, but his manner was arrogant, condescending and combative, almost as if he were thinking: "Where in the world does this little Jew boy from St. Louis get the nerve to offer AT&T a deal?"

About a week after our meeting, deButts informed Diversified that he was rejecting my proposal. I thought to myself: "I offer them $20 million in profits and they say no and proceed with their plans to build their own processing plant in Gaston, South Carolina, at a construction cost of approximately $220 million, plus operating costs after the plant started up, which easily could have run into millions. How dumb can these people be?" I also had warned deButts that those enormous freight costs would eventually sink the Gaston project. And I was exactly right because AT&T eventually shut down the entire Gaston operation. He should have listened to this high school dropout because I could have saved him millions.

When deButts said no to Diversified's proposal, I decided to seek relief in the courts. I knew that to go up against a monolithic, monopolistic company like AT&T would require massive balls and a deep belief in yourself. And, believe me, I had both.

Before taking legal action, I took one more shot at getting back AT&T's business by contacting Zane Barnes, a friend who was president of Southwestern Bell, one of AT&T's larger subsidiaries which operated the phone service in five states.

Barnes, who frequently played tennis at my home, told me he had to follow orders and could not send his plastic insulated wire to Diversified's processing plants. "Benny," he said, "my hands are tied on this one. All my materials have to go straight to our processing plant in Gaston." To me, this was further proof of how AT&T was squeezing us right out of the business and monopolizing it for themselves.

Now was the time to sue, I thought. I tried to hire a large, high-powered law firm in Washington, D.C. I wanted that firm to take our case on a contingency basis, but they wouldn't go for it and turned me down because AT&T "would spend everyone into oblivion."

So, I went to a smaller St. Louis law firm, Guilfoil, Petzall & Shoemake, the 12th largest law firm in our city—a firm which had handled numerous legal matters for Diversified over the years. They agreed to take the case on a contingency basis, along with some up front money.

Finally, on October 26, 1978, Diversified Industries filed suit against AT&T and two of its large subsidiaries, Western Electric and Nassau Recycle Corp. Our suit accused the three companies of violating the

Federal Judge H. Kenneth Wangelin
THE ST. LOUIS MERCANTILE LIBRARY AT THE UNIVERSITY OF MISSOURI ST. LOUIS

Sherman Anti-Trust Act and asked for damages of $100 million to be tripled to $300 million under the terms of the anti-trust laws.

The suit was filed in the U.S. District Court for the Eastern District of Missouri. Federal Judge H. Kenneth Wangelin, who had a reputation for being a very fair jurist with an abundance of common sense, presided over the case.

In my mind, this lawsuit was really Benny versus Goliath, because we were taking on not only the largest non-industrial company in the world—only the oil giants Exxon and Royal Dutch Shell were bigger—but AT&T was also a company that had immensely deep pockets, political influence in the highest levels of the U.S. Government, and a huge legal team that included more than 250 attorneys.

In short, AT&T was a colossus. AT&T's sales were almost $70 billion while ours were just $142 million. This meant we were taking on a company that was 500 times our size in terms of sales. We were like an ant attacking an elephant, but this ant had guts and perseverance—and in the end, it was proven that our cause was legally just.

The focus of our lawsuit was to utilize a pistol strategy rather than a blanket shotgun effort. To make it easy for the jury to understand, we zeroed in only on the specific aspects of our case. We didn't make even one single amendment to our case, which was highly unusual.

The suit evolved into a blizzard of paperwork. It lasted more than 5$^1/_2$ years, with 441 depositions taken, an ungodly number because in a case like ours, 20 to 30 depositions would have usually been sufficient.

Because of the complexities of this case, it took five years—until September 26, 1983—before the jury began to hear testimony.

During those five years, both parties were taking depositions at a record pace, were engaged in preparing various other documents, traveled tens of thousands of miles and spent thousands of hours producing and selecting evidence.

As evidence of AT&T's deep pockets, they produced four expert witnesses and paid them a total of $2.5 million for their work. In contrast, Diversified had just one expert witness who was paid a fraction of what the AT&T experts got.

Five years of preparation by both sides produced 1.25 million of pages of documents, which stacked one on top of each other would add up to a column nearly 500 feet high. Our law firm spent 35,000 hours on the case.

To handle this blizzard of paperwork, Diversified rented space in the same building as its corporate headquarters—a strategy which made things run more smoothly and more seamlessly in our prosecution of AT&T, and which, I believe, greatly helped in the winning of our case.

More importantly, we hired two document experts, Oscar Beldner and Henry Rathert, both of whom were former IRS employees who could spot things a layman would never uncover. Beldner, whose son, Rick, was Diversified's general counsel, was known among his colleagues as a no-nonsense Eliot Ness type who had worked for the U.S. Justice Department relentlessly hunting down organized crime figures. When Oscar and Henry went to Florida to review AT&T documents, the company would not permit them to enter their building but made them work from an unairconditioned, broiling trailer on their parking lot. But turning up the heat on Oscar and Henry backfired. It only made the pair more determined to do an excellent job, which they did.

OSCAR BELDNER WAS ABSOLUTELY INCORRUPTIBLE. IN THE EARLY 1970S, I WAS IN LAS VEGAS GAMBLING—WHAT ELSE?— WHEN I RAN INTO OSCAR WHO WAS IN VEGAS AS A MEMBER OF THE ORGANIZED CRIME STRIKE FORCE. I ASKED OSCAR OUT TO DINNER. HE SAID NO. THEN I ASKED HIM TO HAVE COFFEE WITH ME THE NEXT MORNING AND HE RELUCTANTLY AGREED. THE NEXT MORNING, I WAS SEATED IN THE COFFEE SHOP SURROUNDED BY SEVERAL VERY CLOSE FRIENDS. OSCAR WALKED INTO THE COFFEE SHOP, SAW THE PEOPLE I WAS HAVING BREAKFAST WITH—THEN WHEELED QUICKLY AROUND AND LEFT. I RAN OUTSIDE THE COFFEE SHOP AND GRABBED OSCAR'S ARM. BEFORE I COULD SAY ONE WORD, OSCAR WAS ALL OVER ME: "BEN, NOT ONLY CAN I NOT HAVE COFFEE WITH YOU, BUT ALL OF THOSE PEOPLE YOU ARE SEATED WITH ARE GOING TO BE INDICTED BY THE GOVERNMENT. SO THANKS FOR THE COFFEE. BUT NO THANKS." THEN OSCAR FLED THE SCENE.

Also essential in furthering our case, was the so-called Black Book, which was written by myself and our executive vice president, Leo Paradoski. The Black Book outlined every facet of our business, laid out our strategies, and demonstrated the beneficial effects of AT&T working with us—and not against us. (In fact, AT&T was such a secretive company that we only learned of their intent to go into the processing business in Gaston though a tiny news release published in a trade magazine. AT&T was like the CIA—the less publicity the better.)

Finally, a jury of six persons was selected to hear our case. In my eyes, it could only be described as a blue-collar jury and I couldn't have been more delighted over its composition, mainly middle-class working people, including a nurse and a janitor.

I thought to myself: "This is the perfect jury." Why? Because every member of this jury had paid his or her monthly phone bill for decades, and I rightly suspected (as the verdict proved) that each member of the jury had an ingrained dislike of the phone company for taking their money for all those years.

The trial lasted for 55 days and I made a point of attending every single day. I always sat in the front row of the spectators' section, and I usually had on an inexpensive, well-worn, plain brown suit, leaving my expensive custom-made blue "tycoon" suits at home in my closet.

I wanted to show the jury that I was one of them. But more importantly, I wanted that jury to be able to attach a human face to the man whose company had been ruined by the steamroller that was AT&T.

To this day, I fervently believe that my constant presence in the courtroom was a psychological ploy that created a sympathetic link between myself and that jury. It couldn't have hurt; it could have only helped our case.

In fact, every day a little African American, who was on the jury

ST. LOUIS BUSINESS
JOURNAL
ST. LOUIS, MO.
W. 16,213

MAR 12 1984

Investors bet Diversified will win

suit vs. AT&T

By ROBERT MELNICK

Investors are betting that Diversified Industries Inc. will win its lawsuit against American Telephone & Telegraph Co. Diversified's stock price rose from a low of $3⅞ to a high of $6 during the weeks preceding the decision.

The volume traded has increased similarly during the period. On March 6, the date the case was sent to the jury, 57,600 shares were traded on the New York Stock Exchange. That represents a twelvefold increase from the

Officials at Diversified said they did not know the reason for the rise in the stock's price or volume traded.

Stock analysts in New York attribute the rise in price and volume to Diversified's antitrust suit. "Some lawyers must think the case is going to be won by Diversified," said Mort Segal, an analyst with Value Line Inc.

Diversified claims, in the suit filed in 1978, that AT&T and two of its subsidiaries forced Diversified out of the wire processing business. Diversified seeks $100 million in damages, to be trebled under the provisions of the Clayton Antitrust Act.

The principal activity of Diversified is metals trading. The St. Louis-based firm also reclaims precious and semi-precious metals and produces brass strip, markets structural steel and processes high temperature alloys. The firm had sales of $142 million last year.

AT&T, with 1983 revenues of $69.4 billion, has gone to great lengths to defend itself in the suit.

For the last several months, AT&T has rented 20 to 50 rooms nightly at the

Diversified Stock

Date	Volume traded	Closing price
3/6	57,600	$5.50
3/5	57,800	$5.875
3/2	31,300	$5.25
3/1	18,200	$4.50
2/29	6,800	$4.375
2/28	8,300	$4.375
2/27	14,500	$4.375
2/24	11,100	$4.125
2/23	11,100	$4.00
2/22	4,600	$4.125

This chart shows the volume of shares traded and the closing stock price of Diversified Industries Inc. for the period leading up to the Diversified vs. AT&T lawsuit. The case was sent to the jury on Mar. 6.

Source: Stifel, Nicolaus & Co. Inc. and The Wall Street Journal.

4,600 shares traded two weeks earlier, on February 22.

—and had been a janitor like myself—would walk right by me in my front seat and wink directly at me. Those daily winks could only mean one of two things: "I am going to get you, you son-of-a-bitch," or else "Don't worry about a thing. Your case looks good to me." I'm positive he meant the latter. To me, the "winking janitor" was on our side.

As for myself, I couldn't wait to testify about how AT&T went into the processing business and cut off 65 percent of our raw materials. When I was called as a witness, I testified for two full days.

Those were two rewarding but often difficult days on the witness stand. The lawyers AT&T had engaged were smart. They were always trying to cross me up to find holes and misstatements in my testimony. They would take a statement I had uttered and try and turn it against me to make me look like a fool who didn't know what he was talking about.

But they were fucking with the wrong person. I knew my facts and figures down to the last decimal point. I would think deeply before answering their questions. I knew exactly what I had testified to, and I wouldn't give them an inch of a chance of questioning my expertise. I gave their lawyers a very hard time, and I made damn certain they were not going to put me in the trick bag. They may have had tons of law degrees going for them, but I had some powerful ammunition, too. It's called street smarts.

To put it plainly, AT&T lawyers were hoist by their own petard. That's a French expression that means the bomb they tried to set for me blew up in their own faces instead.

As an example of their stupidity, their lawyers made the mistake of questioning me about memos—all headlined in Yiddish—which were written to me by a Diversified employee who fancied himself an expert in Yiddish.

When I was asked how I knew what the Yiddish memos meant,

ST. LOUIS POST-DISPATCH   Sat., Mar. 10, 1984

Firm Wins $105 Million From AT&T

**By Paul Wagman
and Kathryn Rogers**
Of the Post-Dispatch Staff

A federal jury here has ordered American Telephone & Telegraph Co. to pay $105 million to Diversified Industries Inc. of St. Louis because AT&T monopolized the scrap copper business.

The jury's actual award was $35 million. But because damages in anti-trust cases are by law automatically tripled, the award is $105 million — the largest in the history of the U.S. District Court here, court observers said.

"I love the jury system," Ben Fixman, founder and chairman of Diversified, exclaimed in the hall outside the courtroom after the verdict was read. "It took 5½ years, but we got our day in court."

AT&T's attorneys were visibly downcast. They said they were surprised by both the verdict and the size of the judgment. An AT&T spokesman said the company "will immediately ask the judge to set aside the verdict — and if he does not do so, we will appeal." U.S. District Judge H. Kenneth Wangelin presided over the trial.

Ben Fixman
Diversified Industries chairman

For Diversified, the verdict represented a storybook ending to a struggle that the firm liked to portray as David versus Goliath.

Diversified trades metals, makes

See AT&T, Page 12

AT&T opened a convenient door for me and I barged right on in.

Their line of questioning provided me with the opportunity to lay my Horatio Alger story on the jury. I testified about my youth as a poverty-stricken boy who was raised by an immigrant mother who only spoke Yiddish to me until I was 13, when she learned enough English to become a U.S. citizen.

I testified about my poor mother working as a domestic for as little as a dollar a day, cleaning homes. I told the jury about our family being on relief and having to buy a 10-cent loaf of bread on credit. I testified about selling newspapers at age 7 to help support our family. I told them about having to drop out of high school as a freshman and going to work as a janitor. Realizing they had made a mistake, the AT&T lawyers objected to my testimony, but Judge Wangelin overruled them by uttering just one sentence: "Counselor, you opened the door."

At another point in the trial, the judge became aggravated at an AT&T lawyer who was dragging out the proceedings. The judge told the lawyer: "Counselor, unless you are the lead mule in the mule train, your view of the world doesn't change very much."

I may have been biased, but as I told my story I could almost feel in the courtroom a sense of wonderment. I know it had a powerful and positive effect on the jurors. I also helped our case in another meaningful way. Leo Paradoski, our executive vice president, testified about the volume that AT&T's business represented. It was 65 percent and that was crucial to our case. The AT&T attorney who questioned Leo was skillful and his questions rattled Leo a bit and confused him. When the judge called a recess for lunch, I analyzed the situation and demonstrated to Leo how AT&T's numbers made absolutely no sense at all. Leo then went back on the witness stand, and using my analysis, buttressed his testimony and made it much clearer and stronger to the jury. And under redirect examination, Leo's testimony was even more convincing, a definite plus for our side.

When Judge Wangelin sent the case to the jury, they deliberated for 18 hours over three days. Then on day two of the deliberations, the jurors asked to see Diversified's Black Book. Neither side objected to this, so the Black Book was given to the jury. Outside in the hallway, I was ecstatic. I grabbed my attorney Jim Shoemake and said: "Jim, we've won our case. We've got them by the balls."

And on March 9, 1984, the jury awarded Diversified $105 million, plus costs estimated by knowledgeable attorneys at up to $30 million. The size of the verdict against AT&T was one of the largest ever awarded in the history of the State of Missouri.

AS THE CASE PROGRESSED, I REJECTED SEVERAL OFFERS TO SETTLE FROM AT&T. I TOLD THEM TO SHOVE IT WHEN THEY OFFERED ME $8 MILLION. THEY THEN WENT TO $10 MILLION (ANOTHER NO), $25 MILLION (NO AGAIN) AND FINALLY $45 MILLION (NO THANKS). THESE REJECTIONS WERE DRIVING OUR LAWYERS CRAZY, BUT I DIDN'T CARE BECAUSE MY GUT FEELINGS TOLD ME TO BE PATIENT BECAUSE WE WERE SITTING ON A BIG WINNER.

"I love the jury system," I told a *St. Louis Post-Dispatch* reporter afterwards. "It took 5½ years but we got our day in court."

Inwardly, I teared up after hearing the decision. I just felt exuberant because I knew in my mind that AT&T—besides being the loser in the lawsuit—was a company that had anti-Semitic tendencies, and it gave me great pleasure to know that these so-called genius executives of AT&T had tried in vain to fuck a little Jew boy from St. Louis. For their efforts they got their asses handed to them.

THE AFTERMATH: NEVER COUNT
YOUR CHICKENS BEFORE THEY HATCH

As expected, AT&T appealed the decision to the United States 8th Circuit Court of Appeals. (Diversified was not entitled to any money until all appeals had been exhausted.)

Meanwhile, there was a case pending before the United States Supreme Court known as the Copperweld Case. The issue the court was deciding was whether a parent company and its wholly owned subsidiary are two separate and distinct entities capable of conspiring with each other. On June 19, 1984—several months after Diversified had won its case—the Supreme Court decided in a 5-3 decision that a parent and a subsidiary are NOT corporate entities for the purpose of conspiring with each other to violate the law.

That Supreme Court decision was a real body blow to Diversified because our anti-trust suit was based on our argument that AT&T conspired with all of its wholly owned operating subsidiaries to control the supply of copper wire for recycling purposes.

As a result of the Supreme Court's Copperweld decision, the 8th U.S. Circuit Court of Appeals would have been required to apply the law to AT&T's appeal. In all likelihood that would have resulted in overturning all or a major part of the jury verdict in Diversified's favor because we would no longer be able to show there were two independent parties who conspired to violate the anti-trust law.

Besides the possibility of a reduction in our award, the Copperweld decision had other severe consequences. It meant that the case could conceivably drag on for years and years because of almost endless appeals, with Diversified absorbing huge and ongoing legal costs.

Considering all these issues—especially the probability that our award would be substantially reduced—Diversified's board of directors

**WOOSTER, OHIO
RECORD
D. 25,860**

MAR 10 1984

AT&T Ordered To Pay $105 Million In Antitrust Award

ST. LOUIS (UPI) — A federal court jury has ordered American Telephone & Telegraph Co. to pay a $105 million damage award to Diversified Industries in a 5-year-old antitrust suit judgment.

The verdict was returned Friday in the fourth day of jury deliberations, which took a total of 18 hours, in the 54-day trial that spanned nearly six months.

The six jurors found that AT&T violated several provisions of the Sherman Antitrust Act. The jury awarded Diversified damages of $35 million on its claim that the telecommunications giant sought to take over the "wire chopping" business of recovering copper from discarded telephone cables.

However, a total of $105 million was awarded because of provisions of the Clayton Antitrust Act that treble the amount of damages. Diversified had sought $80 million, which would have been $240 million.

Senior U.S. District Judge H. Kenneth Wangelin presided over the lengthy trial, which included the emotional testimony of Diversified founder and Chairman Ben Fixman.

Fixman had testified he invented a chopping process that economically and efficiently separates the insulating covering from the wire. The firm then resold the copper.

After the verdict was reached, Fixman said, "If the money from the verdict is received, it will be a base upon which the company will be able to expand its activities."

He noted the $105 million would be reduced by substantial attorneys' fees.

DIVERSIFIED, A metals company based in St. Louis, charged that AT&T deliberately put it out of the wire-recycling business. Diversified once was a major recycler of copper telephone wire received from Nassau Recycle Corp., a subsidiary of AT&T's Western Electric Co.

Diversified said Western and Nassau executives violated antitrust laws by "restrictive, in-house dealing practices" that limited the supply of insulated copper wire to Diversified.

Nassau subcontracted with Diversified to process its wire, but built its own processing plant in Gaston, S.C. Diversified charged that Bell instructed its 23 telephone systems to sell scrap only to Nassau, thus cutting off Diversified's scrap supply.

Diversified said it was forced to close three of its plants in 1977 and lay off 200 workers. The plants were in suburban Hazelwood, Tamaqua, Pa., and Cucamonga, Calif.

AT&T attorneys argued during the trial that Diversified closed the plants because the wire recycling business was unprofitable and because Diversified Metals, its recycling subsidiary, was one of Diversified's weakest parts.

AT&T said that from 1970 to 1977, Diversified Metals made a profit only in 1973 and 1974. AT&T also said it let hundreds of bids for scrap wire since 1977, when it opened Nassau's South Carolina plant, and that Diversified subsidaries won some of them.

Wooster Ohio Record reports the outcome, March 10, 1984

decided to settle with AT&T for a sum in excess of $40 million.

The whole thing reinforced my belief that in business, you can't count your chickens before they hatch.

Despite Copperweld, I still had the satisfaction of knowing in my own mind that we had beaten AT&T in court in a 5½ year legal battle that proved a relatively small company like ours could get its day in court and come out a winner against a giant monopoly.

It's interesting to note that after we won the case, AT&T quickly settled 54 other outstanding lawsuits pending against them.

I think it's fair to say that Diversified Industries led the way in proving to the world that AT&T was a bad corporate citizen and a monopolistic predator. CU

CHAPTER EIGHT

HELLO, GOLDA, MOSHE, AND ABBA
(Benny, this time bring some big bread and
we don't mean a *challah* (a braided white bread.)

Over the years, I had many trips to Israel, sometimes taking my family, sometimes going alone, sometimes in the company of other Jewish CEOs.

In 1967, right after the second Battle of Mitla Pass in the Sinai, I was invited by the Israeli government to view the destruction the Israelis had wrought on the panicked and run-away Egyptian forces.

As I walked on the battlefield where the Jews had triumphed, I could not believe my eyes. As far as I could see, there were soaring piles of destroyed tanks, blown-up troop carriers and mangled vehicles of every kind that once were the pride of the Egyptian Army.

I even saw hundreds and hundreds of pairs of shoes, maybe as many as thousands of pairs of shoes, left behind by the Egyptian soldiers in their haste to run from the battlefield and save their lives. This battlefield of twisted and wrecked armor was a powerful tribute to the might of the Israeli Army and Air Force.

(Years later, in 1972, right after the "Yom Kippur War," I traveled to Israel again and saw mountains of destroyed weaponry that once carried Arab banners. In the "Yom Kippur War," the Arabs were estimated to have lost more than 2,000 tanks and over 400 planes, another testament to the outnumbered Israelis' determination to survive despite being surrounded by the most hostile of enemies who wanted to make Israel perish from the earth.)

But the trip I made to Israel in 1969 was not to tour battlefields. It had a far more important objective. After fighting and winning three major wars, Israel had depleted its assets and was in catastrophic financial shape.

So a desperate call for help went out to 30 American businessmen who were known as big givers. Leading the group was Detroit's Max Fisher, the founder of Marathon Oil Company. Max had been a trusted adviser to

This picture of Israeli Premier Yitzhak Rabin (center) was taken in St. Louis. Rabin, a Nobel Peace Prize winner, was assassinated on Nov. 4, 1995 by a young right-wing Israeli radical. At the far left is Morris Shenker, an attorney known for his defense of Teamsters boss James R. Hoffa. Shenker, who once owned The Dunes Hotel and Casino in Las Vegas, died in 1989. Morris and I were the closest of friends. We both took pride in raising money for Jewish causes.

several U. S. presidents, starting with Dwight D. Eisenhower. He was the elder statesman of North American Jewry and a leading world philanthropist.

To be in the company of such people boggled my mind and opened my purse strings to the tune of giving hundreds of thousands of dollars to the State of Israel. But more than that, the Israeli trip taught me about the valor, strength and determination of the Israelis and made me realize that these were indeed, God's Chosen People.

On the first day of my trip,

Abba Eban, Foreign Minister of Israel (1966–74)

I was given a briefing by the Israeli Chief of Staff, Chaim Bar-Lev. On Day 2, I was briefed by a true Israeli hero, Defense Minister Moshe Dayan. Everything I had read about Dayan made me believe he was a super-aggressive hawk. But after we talked, my impression of Dayan changed. He impressed me with a sincere desire for peace so that Israel could continue its task of building a nation that could thrive despite being surrounded by barbaric enemies who wanted to push the Jews into the sea.

After the Dayan meeting, our group had lunch with Prime Minister Golda Meir and nearly all of the Israeli Cabinet. I thought to myself: "What a wonderful country America is. Here I am, a poor ghetto kid from St. Louis and now I am having lunch with Golda Meir, one of the most respected and revered women in the entire world."

*Letters and the invitation leading up to my trip and dinner with
Foreign Minister Abba Eban.*

Afterward, Israel's Iron Lady—who was battling cancer at the time—and I had a lengthy conversation. This strong-willed, straight-talking grandmother of the Jewish people and I quickly started talking on a "Golda and Ben basis." It was as if we had known each other for years. "Ben," she said, "what Jew wants to go to another Jew and ask for help?" It's a *shonda* (a shame). Then I remembered a quotation she was famous for: "The Muslims can fight and lose, then come back and fight again. But Israel can only lose once?"

My good friend, attorney Morris Shenker
THE ST. LOUIS MERCANTILE LIBRARY AT THE UNIVERSITY OF MISSOURI ST. LOUIS

In Judaism, *chai* (life) is the lucky number 18 and gifts to charity are routinely given in multiples of 18. Before I went to Israel I had decided to add four zeros to 18 and give $180,000 in aid, but Golda's logic and force of personality made me double 18 and add four zeros, and I made a $360,000 contribution to the State of Israel, no small sum back in 1969.

The final and crowning event of my trip was attending a dinner hosted in the home of Foreign Minister Abba Eban. Eban was by far the most eloquent speaker I had ever heard. He noted that 6 million Jews had died in the Holocaust and called for the Arabs to sit down with us like brothers and work out a solution of benefit to Jews, Arabs and all of mankind.

Senator Hubert Humphrey was a good friend and a frequent guest in my home when he visited St. Louis. "Horatio" was a great Vice-President, and it's a shame he lost to Nixon in 1968. He would have made a wonderful President.

My wife, Marilyn, the most magnificent woman I have ever known.

PLATE 2 • THE BEN FIXMAN STORY

A nice honor: *Scrap Age* magazine selected me as its "Man of the Century."

The American Jewish Committee
National Human Relations Award

to

BEN FIXMAN

The American Jewish Committee is privileged to present its 1971 National Human Relations Award to Ben Fixman, a distinguished industrialist whose career has been marked by an abiding desire to help his fellow human beings.

In his rise from impoverished beginnings to business and financial success, Ben Fixman has never forgotten the less fortunate or those in need of a helping hand. He views communal service as an obligation and philanthropy as a sacred trust. He was Chairman of the 1970 Jewish Federation Fund Drive in St. Louis. He is a member of the Advisory Committee of the American Jewish Committee's St. Louis Chapter. Among the other causes he has aided are State of Israel Bonds and the Anti-Defamation League of B'nai B'rith.

He and Mrs. Fixman have been honored for their communal leadership by B'nai B'rith and Bonds for Israel, and were awarded a citation from the State of Israel for their efforts on behalf of Jewish survival.

We of the American Jewish Committee are proud to honor this warm and compassionate humanitarian and to have his name linked with ours in the effort to drive prejudice from the works and heart of man. We present him with this award in the knowledge that men often emulate those whom they honor.

PRESENTED AT A DINNER IN HIS HONOR
ST. LOUIS

October 31, 1971

In 1971, I was named the recipient of the American Jewish Committee's National Human Relations Award. Sen. Hubert Humphrey was kind enough to insert my entire speech in The Congressional Record.

PLATE 4 • THE BEN FIXMAN STORY

The
HUMANITIES
AWARD

ST. LOUIS, MISSOURI

The Humanities Award *recognizes that citizen whose entire life truly reflects the universal aspiration of mankind toward the Fatherhood of God and the Brotherhood of Man. For 1983 it is awarded to*

Ben Fixman

Compassionate Philanthropist
Vigorous Industrialist
Concerned Patriot

Ben Fixman, *a respected businessman and successful entrepreneur, is a deliberate exemplar of the blessing it is to be able to live in America.*

He is working proof that the American dream is alive and well late in the 20th century. Born in St. Louis' old Kerry Patch area, he began work selling newspapers when he was six and he now heads one of the major industrial corporations in the United States.

He literally rose from rags to riches after dropping out of school to help his widowed immigrant mother raise four other children.

A courageous and patriotic American, Ben Fixman has been honored by the State of Israel for his "exceptional service" in the cause of Jewish survival.

Ben Fixman is a compassionate man whose hardships in his early years imbued within him the desire to help others, without regard to race, religion or creed.

He has for many years given unselfishly and unstintingly to those in need. His quiet generosity has earned him the distinction of being known as the philanthropist who refuses to discuss his philanthropies.

Ben Fixman is known for establishing The Marilyn Fixman Cancer Center—Washington University at Jewish Hospital in memory of his beloved wife. He has also reached into his pocket to help the mentally retarded, the sick, the aged, and the chemically dependent.

In tribute *to his outstanding achievements, the Humanities Award is conferred upon Ben Fixman this twenty-fifth day of December 1983.*

ARCHBISHOP OF ST. LOUIS
REPRESENTING INTER-FAITH CLERGY COUNCIL
PRESIDENT, ST. LOUIS RABBINICAL ASSOCIATION
EDITORIAL PAGE EDITOR, ST. LOUIS GLOBE-DEMOCRAT
PUBLISHER, ST. LOUIS GLOBE-DEMOCRAT

In 1983, I was named the winner of the coveted St. Louis Globe-Democrat *Humanities Award. The newspaper's management couldn't believe that I sold the* Globe *when I was a 7-year-old kid.*

One of the six LeRoy Neiman pictures that were stolen from me.

PLATE 6 • THE BEN FIXMAN STORY

Another of the LeRoy Neiman pictures that were stolen.

PRODUCTS DIVERSIFIED MADE

Nuggets®—high purity copper and aluminum

Electrobriqs™— compressed copper Nuggets®

Alumabrigs™— compressed aluminum Nuggets®

Zinc base die-casting metals

Type metals for use in Linotype and Monotype casting

Caulking leads for use in plumbing

PLATE 8 • THE BEN FIXMAN STORY

*Minibriqs®—
compressed copper
Nuggets®*

*Copper Briquets—#1
copper for fire refined
ingots and cathodes*

*Flakes—thin copper
or aluminum products
for specialized use*

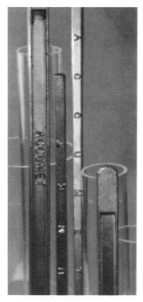

*Solders for use in
electrical, electronic
and metalworking*

*Plastics—Polyvinyl
Chloride and Polyethylene
are a by-product of the
"Cold Process"*

*Speciality Products—
such as Mossy Zinc,
Alloy coatings,
Babbitts, etc.*

Shortly thereafter, the so-called "Lawyer for the Mob," Morris Shenker, arranged a meeting in St. Louis between myself and Yitzhak Rabin, the man who would succeed Mrs. Meir as Prime Minister. Rabin, the winner of the Nobel Peace Prize, died at the hands of an assassin in 1995.

When I visited Israel, I went to Yad Vashem, the memorial for the 6 million Jews who perished in Nazi concentration camps. I said *Kaddish* there and cried my eyes out.

I used my visit to Yad Vashem to drive home a point in a speech I made a year later as the 1970 General Chairman of the Jewish Federation of St. Louis. I told the supporters of the Federation that "Yad Vashem was built by the same people who wanted to forget, but who knew that in order for Judaism to survive, their children must be made to remember what it means to be a Jew, what it means to suffer as a Jew, what it means to be a Jew chosen to suffer."

Before Marilyn passed away, she and I had been honored for "communal leadership" by B'nai B'rith and Bonds for Israel, and the State of Israel delivered a citation for "our efforts on behalf of Jewish survival."

At this point in my life, one honor seemed to follow another. In 1971, the American Jewish Committee named me the recipient of its National Human Relations Award. (See plate 3) This honor put me in some serious company. The two previous winners of this award were Edgar Speer, president of United States Steel Corp., and Willard Rockwell Jr., chairman of the board of North American Rockwell Corp.

In connection with this award, a large dinner was held in St. Louis. Among those attending were keynote speaker Senator Hubert Humphrey of Minnesota, Missouri Senator Thomas F. Eagleton and St. Louis Mayor Alfonso J. Cervantes. The toastmaster was my good friend George Jessel. In my speech to the supporters of the American Jewish Committee, I said

*Helping me admire the American Jewish Committee plaque (left to right)
are famed criminal lawyer Morris Shenker, Missouri Senator Thomas F.
Eagleton, Minnesota Senator Hubert Humphrey, noted St. Louisan
Richard Yalem, and St. Louis Mayor Alfonso J. Cervantes.*

in part: "The task of improving human relations involves hard work in
the years ahead. We have been to the moon, but that really isn't far. For
the greatest distance we have to cover still lies within ourselves."

I also touched on the ongoing crises in the Middle East, saying:
"Even though the people of Israel have lived almost continually in the
shadows of wars and death, they have offered their Arab neighbors the
benefit of their technical knowledge to better their education, to improve
their medical facilities, to find jobs and to raise the efficiencies of their

The Humanities Award

Continued from Page 1A

intended them to be, having a human spirit, possessing pride and dignity, living equally among all men and women."

Sharing the platform with eight former recipients of the award, the 1983 honoree said:

"As I look at the distinguished men and women on this dais and in the audience, I realize that the true humanitarians are not men such as myself, rather, they are men and women who through great self-sacrifice have devoted their lives and their daily existence to a variety of worthwhile causes.

"I like to think that I live in a world where men and women such as myself assist the true humanitarians. We are the means by which they can continue their work. We are the means by which they can bring a ray of hope to a shattered dream. We are the means that make their commitment, their dreams and their hopes possible."

FIXMAN, BORN to poverty on the North Side, rose to prominence as founder, chairman and chief executive officer of Diversified Industries Inc.

There to pay tribute to him were Joseph A. Simpkins, who received the Humanities Award in 1972; the Rev. Fred L. Zimmerman, S.J., 1974; Martin L. Mathews, 1975; I.E. Millstone, 1976; Monsignor Elmer H. Behrmann, 1977; John H. Londoff, 1978; Oliver W. Langhorst, 1980; and the Rev. William G. Gillespie, 1982.

Also on the platform were members of the selection committee: Archbishop John L. May, Dr. Cyrus S. Keller, president of the Inter-Faith Clergy Council; Rabbi Robert P. Jacobs, executive vice president of the St. Louis Rabbinical Association, representing Rabbi Bruce S. Diamond, president of the St. Louis Rabbinical Association; and Martin L. Duggan, editor of The Globe-Democrat editorial page. Bauman is the fifth member of the committee.

Special greetings were given by Lt. Gov. Kenneth J. Rothman, Mayor Vincent C. Schoemehl Jr. and St. Louis County Executive Gene McNary.

BAUMAN, INTRODUCING Fixman, recounted highlights of the honoree's life and special honors he has received in recognition of his charitable contributions regardless of race or creed.

"The very first people he helped," Bauman said, "were a group of nuns in Kerry Patch. He never forgot that they gave him lunch every day when he was a young boy. He was so poor that the price of a daily lunch, 5 cents, was more than he usually had in his pockets.

"Because of his willingness to share his wealth with the needy and to share it in a non-ostentatious way, he has received many honors. One of the most significant came in 1971, when he was named as the recipient of the National Human Relations Award of the American Jewish Committee."

Bauman also referred to a more recent honor, a citation by the St. Louis Rabbinical College for outstanding service to the Jewish community. Fixman received the college's Keser Torah award in recognition of his work in the Jewish community at the 21st annual Keser Torah banquet Nov. 13.

THE PUBLISHER also cited Fixman as the prime mover in the establishment of the Jewish Community Centers' Camp Sabra and a generous donor, through his company, to the Jesuit Program for Living and Learning.

"He was also the leading force behind the establishment of the Marilyn Fixman Cancer Center at Jewish Hospital, a center created to help cancer patients survive the disease which caused the death of his wife, Marilyn," Bauman said.

Fixman responded:

"It was during Marilyn's illness that many men and women of good faith, true humanitarians all, continually went out of their way to offer us comfort and hope in trying to eliminate despair from our lives.

"That experience, more than any other, taught me that caring people can restore hope to a cause seemingly lost, that caring people can bring comfort to the suffering, that caring people can bring the promise of better things to come.

"IT IS IN Marilyn's memory that I choose to continue much of my efforts. It is for my daughters and their families that I hope to set as example, to show by deed that we as a family have an obligation to share what we can, that we as a family will always pray for miracles, that all men and women have the opportunity to share this nation's bountiful fruits in peace and freedom."

Fixman returned the $1,000 check that goes with the award to Bauman, asking that it be contributed to the Salvation Army.

The publisher concluded his tribute to the recipient by reading the traditional parchment, which cited Fixman as a "compassionate philanthropist, vigorous industrialist, concerned patriot" and read, in part:

"Ben Fixman, a respected businessman and successful entrepreneur, is a deliberate exemplar of the blessing it is to be able to live in America ... working proof that the American dream is alive and well in the 20th century."

Globe-Democrat
Photos by
Paul Ockrassa

The HUMANITIES AWARD

ST. LOUIS, MISSOURI

The Humanities Award recognizes those citizens whose actions truly reflect the universal aspirations of mankind toward the Fatherhood of God and the Brotherhood of Man. For 1983 it is awarded to

Ben Fixman
Compassionate Philanthropist
Vigorous Industrialist
Concerned Patriot

Ben Fixman, a respected businessman and successful entrepreneur is a deliberate exemplar of the blessing it is to be able to live in America ...

The Humanities Award

Past recipients of the Humanities Award listen to the speeches Wednesday. From left are Joseph A. Simpkins; the Rev. Fred L. Zimmerman, S.J.; Martin L. Mathews; I.E. Millstone; the Rt. Rev Msgr. Elmer H. Behrmann; John H. Londoff; Ollie W. Langhorst and the Rev. William G. Gillespie.

Flanked by civic leaders and past recipients of the Humanities Award, Ben Fixman delivers his acceptance speech Wednesday.

Receiving the Globe-Democrat *Humanities Award, part 2*

The New York Times masthead clipping:

The New York Times

"All the News That's Fit to Print"

A Scrapper from St. Louis — **MAN IN BUSINESS**

A New Horatio Alger Tale

By GERALD J. MEYER

"I had a chip on my shoulder, to tell you the truth. I had to prove to myself that I was as good as the people who had ... a formal education. I was driven."

ST. LOUIS—Ben Fixman is the kind of man about whom Horatio Alger wrote those success stories. He started working at the age of 6, dropped out of school to help his widowed mother, and now at 45 is chairman of one of the largest corporations in America. He would not seem to have many things to regret.

But Mr. Fixman does admit to regretting one thing. He wishes that his company, Diversified Industries, Inc., did not live up to its name so fully. If he could build his business all over again, he says, he would make it much less diversified.

"We started acquiring companies to protect ourselves against economic conditions," Mr. Fixman explained. "Had we known what we know today, we wouldn't have done it. We would have stayed specifically in the metals field without getting into any of the rest of it. From now on, our emphasis is going to be on growth in the metals area. In metals processing technology, we are just at the beginning."

In other words, Diversified Industries, which until last year was known as the Diversified Metals Corporation, and now includes more than 30 separate companies producing everything from ball-point pens to fabrics, is now refocusing its attention on what made all the rest possible—metal.

Mr. Fixman was born in 1925 in the tough Kerry Patch District of St. Louis,

and his father died when he was a year and a half old. His immigrant mother could not speak English, and was barely able to keep her five children from being put into an orphanage.

When he was 6, Mr. Fixman began working after school as a newsboy and later as a janitor. His formal education ended after eight months of high school when he began to work full time for a manufacturer of women's clothing.

"At 21, after becoming assistant to the president of the firm, I left to go into the clothing business for myself with the fortune I'd accumulated," Mr. Fixman recalled, "It was $3,000, and I quickly learned that it was inadequate."

He then bought a truck and began traveling through the Midwest, buying and selling scrap metal. He "went through a period of crisis in the early nineteen-sixties when Mr. Fixman began searching for new ways to get copper from old insulated wire that he bought all over the world. The traditional reclaiming method, burning, was dirty and inefficient, and Mr. Fixman sought a way to remove the insulation mechanically. He invested heavily in research

door to door, and then he returned to the scrap metals business.

Mr. Fixman bought his first scrap yard in 1951. In 1954, with a partner, whom he bought out two years later, he formed the Fischer-Fixman Metals Company. In 1956 Diversified Metals was born, and it grew rapidly, spurred by Mr. Fixman's ambition.

"I had a chip on my shoulder, to tell you the truth," he said. "I had to prove to myself that I was as good as the people who had an opportunity to get a formal education. I was driven. I also had the advantage of being one of the younger men in the scrap business. Most young men don't want to go into the scrap metal business today, and that was true 20 years ago, too. I could see opportunities that my competitors couldn't."

The growing company

and was almost out of money before the company's now famous "cold process" was discovered.

"We didn't think we were going to lick it," Mr. Fixman said. "We were about to go broke — we'd spent half a million dollars and had no results. Strange as it sounds, I thought of the solution in my sleep—that's the gospel truth. I woke up in the middle of the night, 'I've got it.' My wife thought I was crazy."

The process uses a combination of ore-dressing and coal-cleaning machines to separate aluminum, copper and other metals from rubber and plastic insulating material.

From that point, as Mr. Fixman proudly recalled, Diversified "grew by leaps and bounds," expanding, acquiring, reaping profits. The company went public in 1956 and was first listed on the New York Stock Exchange Sept. 10, 1969.

Diversified had heavy losses early this year, but Mr. Fixman confidently predicts profits for the year as a whole. New techniques in metals reclamation now being perfected by the company's research division, he asserted, will be as revolutionary as the cold process was.

Diversified Industries reported a net loss of $3,211,-166 on sales of $92,538,407 for the quarter ended July 31.

For the nine months ended July 31, the company had sales of $259,802,385 and earnings of $1,550,255, or 27 cents a share. Net income for the year that ended last Oct. 31 was $8,146,339.

Mr. Fixman said that he was not surprised by his 20-year transformation from baby chair salesman to captain of industry. "I've been too busy to be surprised," he said. "I have only one major enthusiasm—my work. I enjoy business."

He is not a conspicuous member of St. Louis's commercial or social establishments—"I couldn't care less about that," he said—and he is known for maintaining close friendships with unimportant persons he has known since childhood.

He is a philanthropist who refuses to discuss his philanthropies. His associates speak of him as a man who cannot tolerate inefficiency, who peremptorily fires people he considers unproductive, generously rewards those who are productive and loyal and never forgets or forgives a double-cross.

"I have been accused of being a tyrant," he said. "So be it."

Mr. Fixman and his wife, who live in Ladue, Mo., have three daughters and two granddaughters.

Last year a trade magazine, Scrap Age, named Mr. Fixman its "man of the decade." This year, talking about the honor and about his career, Mr. Fixman explained his success.

"My method is based on engineering," he said. "You solve the problem or you starve."

The New York Times *called my life a "Horatio Alger Tale."*
Whoever wrote that headline hit the mark.

Test your Christmas IQ!
Take the St. Louis Holiday Trivia Quiz and see how much you know about Christmases past in St. Louis. **The Magazine**

Mystery and glitter in the Kingdom of Khorassan
Here's complete coverage of the Veiled Prophet Ball, including a look at the new Queen of Love and Beauty. **Living**

List of the agencies that will receive help from the Old Newsboys fund **9A**

Frigid: Bitterly cold Saturday; high near 5 degrees and low 6 to 12 below zero. Winds up to 25 mph.
Christmas Day: Chance of snow. High 5 to 10 degrees. More weather on 10A

St. Louis Globe-Democrat

131 Years of Public Service / Founded July 1, 1852

Saturday — Sunday
December 24-25, 1983
50¢
Section A — Pages 1-12

Vol. 132 — No. 152

C

Copyright 1983 Globe-Democrat Publishing Co.

Ben Fixman: "To know the feeling of need you have to experience it."

Philanthropist for all people

By MARY KIMBROUGH
Globe-Democrat Staff Writer

He is the stuff of which Horatio Alger fashioned his heroes — the 6-year-old newsboy from the edge of Kerry Patch, scrounging for pennies to supplement the family relief; the son of Russian Jews, born into poverty and fed by neighborhood nuns and the Salvation Army when there was no food at home; the high school drop-out who rose from janitor of a retail chain to assistant to the

Humanities Award

president; the enterprising scrapman who became a corporate executive and founded an industrial empire.

This is Ben Fixman, president, chairman and chief executive officer of Diversified Industries Inc.

This is the founder of the Marilyn Fixman Cancer Center of Jewish Hospital, in memory of his wife, who died in 1980. This is the donor of $250,000 toward the purchase of Camp Sabra of the Jewish Community Centers Association. This is the Jew who has given a residence for boys sheltered and taught in the Jesuit Living and Learning program.

THIS IS THE man who "cannot remember turning down a charitable appeal," who, with his company, has helped meet such divergent needs as the American Italian Earthquake Appeal, the Anti-Drug Abuse Educational Fund, the Foundation for Clinical Research, the National Jewish Hospital/National Asthma Center, United Way, the mentally retarded, the individual unable to pay a utility bill.

And this is the recipient of The Globe-Democrat's 1983 Humanities Award, an honor

Continued on Page 6A

'This very night... your Savior was born'

At that time Emperor Augustus sent out an order for all the citizens of the empire to register themselves for the census. When this first census took place, Quirinius was the governor of Syria. Everyone then went to register himself, each to his own town.

Joseph went from the town of Nazareth, in Galilee, to Judea, to the town named Bethlehem, where King David was born. Joseph went there because he himself was a descendant of David. He went to register himself with Mary, who was promised in marriage to him.

She was pregnant, and while they were in Bethlehem, the time came for her to have her baby. She gave birth to her first son, wrapped him in cloths and laid him in a manger — there was no room for them to stay in the inn.

Good morning news

There were some shepherds in that part of the country who were spending the night in the fields, taking care of their flocks. An angel of the Lord appeared to them, and the glory of the Lord shone over them. They were terribly afraid, but the angel said to them: "Don't be afraid! For I am here with good news for you, which will bring great joy to all the people. This very night in David's town your Savior was born — Christ the Lord! This is what will prove it to you: you will find a baby wrapped in cloths and lying in a manger."

Suddenly a great army of heaven's angels appeared with the angel, singing praises to God:

"Glory to God in the highest heaven!

And peace on earth to men with whom he is pleased!"

When the angels went away from them back into heaven, the shepherds said to one another, "Let us go to Bethlehem and see this thing that has happened, that the Lord has told us." So they hurried off and found Mary and Joseph, and saw the baby lying in the manger.

When the shepherds saw him they told them what the angel had said about this child. All who heard it were filled with wonder at what the shepherds told them. Mary remembered all these things and thought deeply about them.

The shepherds went back, singing praises to God for all they had heard and seen; it had been just as the angel had told them.

From Good News For Modern Man: The New Testament in Today's English Version originally published by American Bible Society.

Globe-Democrat Photo by Bob Moore

A stained glass window tells the Christmas story. The window is at Mary Queen of Peace Church, 678 Lockwood Ave., Webster Groves.

Ben Fixman: A philanthropist to all

Continued from Page 1A

which annually recognizes "that citizen whose entire life truly reflects the universal aspiration of mankind toward the fatherhood of God and the brotherhood of man."

Established by this newspaper in 1956, the award will be presented to Fixman during ceremonies at 11 a.m. Wednesday in Edison Theater on the Washington University campus. He was selected for the honor by an interfaith committee: Archbishop John L. May; Rabbi Bruce S. Diamond, president of the St. Louis Rabbinical Association and rabbi of Congregational Kol Am; and the Rev. Cyrus S. Keller Sr., president of the Inter-Faith Clergy Council and presiding elder of the St. Louis-Columbia district of the African Methodist Episcopal Church, along with G. Duncan Bauman, publisher of The Globe-Democrat, and Martin L. Duggan, editorial page editor.

THE AWARD, which is accompanied by a $1,000 cash gift, cites the 58-year-old Fixman as "a compassionate philanthropist, vigorous industrialist, concerned patriot," as "working proof that the American dream is alive and well" and as one "whose hardships in his early years imbued within him the desire to help others without regard to race, religion or creed."

The doughty industrialist and feisty flagwaver has a steel spine, a velvet heart and blood that runs red, white and blue. He's the affectionate father of three and the doting grandfather of six, with the mild manner of a Clark Kent, the guts of a Superman, the business brain of a tycoon and the spunk of an entrepreneur.

He isn't concerned about creed or color when he opens his checkbook. He remembers that a half-century ago no one asked him where his folks came from or where he went to church before serving up a nutritious lunch. In fact, one of his first charitable gifts went to the Catholic nuns who fed him when he didn't have a nickel in his pocket and the cupboard at home was bare.

FIXMAN DOESN'T talk much about his giving — the New York Times once called him a "philanthropist who refuses to discuss his philanthropies" — but he isn't shy about discussing his boyhood.

He was born in the 1800 block of Carr Street, the son of immigrants. His father died when Ben was 18 months old. His mother worked as a domestic for $2 a day and Ben was thrown into a world of want from which he would not emerge until young adulthood.

The family had to depend on relief from public and private sources, but they stayed close and the children learned old-fashioned discipline at their mother's knee.

"I think if we had stolen anything or done anything else wrong, she would have killed us," he said with a grin. "She was a strong lady."

None of the children had much formal education because they all had to go to work.

"WHEN I WAS 6," he recalled, "I had my first newspaper corner, in front of The Globe-Democrat.

"Later, I sold papers at Boatmen's Bank, then I would go to the front of the Garrick Theater until 1 or 2 a.m., finish up at the Missouri Mule about 3 or 4 and take the money home to my mother."

Ben can remember earlier days, however, when there wasn't any money to be taken home to his mother and, often, no food on the table. But the North Side nuns made certain the little boy had a good meal every day, and at Christmas he would trot up to the old Coliseum on Washington Avenue for the Salvation Army party — "the only time I ever had a good Christmas dinner."

"That's why," he said, "I have always tried to do something for the Salvation Army."

WITH BEN AND his brother and sisters working, the family got off relief and "had quite a celebration." Feeling somewhat affluent, they moved to the Central West End where Ben finished grammar school and enrolled in Soldan High School. The sense of plenty was short-lived. When his brother became ill, Ben had to quit high school after eight months to help support his mother.

His first job, at Worth's, wasn't prestigious, but it was the right one for the spunky teen-ager. Not only did he advance from janitor to assistant to the president, practically running a family of eight stores, but here he also met Marilyn Schneider, a fellow employee and his future, cherished wife.

They had little money when they married, but Ben was a born survivor, as hungry for success as he earlier had been for a good meal. He had been given his chance to learn merchandising, and he was a quick study.

At 21, he left Worth's, bought a truck and went into the scrap metal business. Ultimately he developed the revolutionary "Cold Process" for reclaiming copper from insulated wire and this invention, in turn, led to establishment of Diversified Industries, a New York Stock Exchange company with eight operating divisions and annual sales of more than $177 million.

IN THE EXECUTIVE suite, Fixman is a natty dresser, but he has never lost his shirtsleeves work ethic. Several years ago he inserted a newspaper ad for employees, heading the copy, "We give a damn!" and offering "a good day's pay for a full day's work." When only 38 accepted jobs, and 27 others who were hired failed to show up the next day, Fixman charged that America is plagued by a "no-work movement sustained by various governmental giveaways, welfare checks, laziness and indifference."

"I think a lot has to be done in America," he recently told The Globe-Democrat. "The last three years have seen dramatic changes which are very good. It had to come. I think this business about welfare and the giveaway programs has got to stop. As far as 'entitlements' are concerned, I think you are 'entitled' to get up in the morning, breathe the air and go out to work."

But he also believes that those who are in need — the blind, the disabled, the old — are, indeed, "entitled" to help, regardless of race or creed, and he digs deep into his pocket to show his own concern.

BECAUSE OF those charitable contributions to so many different organizations and causes, he received the 1971 Human Relations Award from the American Jewish Committee. In his response — published in the Congressional Record — he said, in part:

"My goal, my dream, is to contribute to a world of better human relations — a world which has been enriched by actions of men and women like yourselves, people who have dedicated their lives to creating a better understanding between all religions, all nations and all races.

"This is the kind of world I want my children and your children and their children to grow up in."

And he feels a responsibility, he says, for helping create that world.

"I think everyone has a responsibility not only to himself and to his family but to the community. Without that community, without a belief in our religion, without the benefits society has given us, we would not be where we are."

But then he paused to look back into the world he knew as a 6-year-old newsboy.

"To know the feeling of need," he said, "you have to experience it."

"Some savior," one colleague kidded me.

St. Louis Globe-Democrat

131 Years of Public Service / Founded July 1, 1852

Thursday, December 29, 1983 — 4 Sections — 42 Pages

Humanitarian gives hope to shattered dreams

By MARY KIMBROUGH
Globe-Democrat Staff Writer

The "true humanitarian" chooses the "less-traveled road, the road without promise of riches or recognition, the road of total commitment to his fellow man, the road leading to those less fortunate, the road inhabited by shattered dreams and hopes long dashed."

With these words, Ben Fixman, St. Louis corporate executive and philanthropist, accepted the 1983 Globe-Democrat Humanities Award in ceremonies Wednesday in the Edison Theater at Washington University.

Fixman, introduced by Globe-Democrat Publisher G. Duncan Bauman, is the 25th to be so honored by this newspaper since the tradition was begun in 1959 to recognize "that citizen whose entire life truly reflects the universal aspiration of mankind toward the Fatherhood of God and the Brotherhood of man."

"THE TRUE humanitarian," Fixman said, "sees people as God

Continued on Page 13A

Globe-Democrat Photo by Paul Ockrassa

Globe-Democrat Publisher G. Duncan Bauman, left, presents the Humanities Award Wednesday to Ben Fixman.

At left: Ben Fixman delivers his acceptance speech during the ceremonies honoring him Wednesday. At right: Lt. Gov. Kenneth H. Rothman praises Fixman, far right. Others, seated from left, are   Mayor Vincent C. Schoemehl Jr., St. Louis County Executive Gene McNary and Globe-Democrat Publisher G. Duncan Bauman.

Receiving the Globe-Democrat *Humanities Award*

business industries. How often in history has a victor so surrounded by blood enemies offered an olive branch of peace?"

The brilliant Senator Humphrey inserted my entire speech into the *Congressional Record* (see Appendix A) and further honored me by describing me as "one of America's truly great citizens."

At this time, I was also the subject of feature stories in *The New York Times*, *St. Louis Post-Dispatch* and *St. Louis Globe-Democrat*. The stories were extremely complimentary—almost to the point of being embarrassing, but the reporters did have their facts straight.

One *Post-Dispatch* story said in part: "He is a world traveler, a subject of conversation in high places, a close acquaintance of at least one chief of state, Prime Minister Golda Meir of Israel, and as one of his colleagues said: 'That ain't bad for a junkman.'"

In 1983, I was named the recipient of the *St. Louis Globe-Democrat* Humanities Award. (See plate 4) The story ran on page one on Christmas Day, and the headline on a Christmas story that ran right next to mine read: "This very night your Savior was born." Boy, did I take a lot of ribbing about that from my friends. "Some savior," one colleague kidded me.

The *Globe* story was headlined: "Philanthropist for All People." When I told the *Globe* reporter that I had sold their paper when I was a 7-year-old kid to bring some money into my family, the paper went overboard with their praise. It was almost too much. But, in truth, what person in the world doesn't like to hear nice things said about him?

The first paragraph of the *Globe* story read this way: "He is the stuff of which Horatio Alger fashioned his heroes—the 7-year-old newsboy scrounging for pennies to help out his family, which was on relief; the son of Russian Jews, born into poverty and fed by neighborhood nuns and the Salvation Army when there was no food at home; the high school dropout who rose from janitor of a retail chain to assistant to the

Our Cover . . . "Man of the Century"

Ben Fixman

Chairman of the Board
Diversified Industries, Inc.

As Ben Fixman has often said: "I've already had enough praise in my lifetime."

But there was still do doubt that Ben was immeasurably pleased at having been selected as a "Man of The Century" by Scrap Age Magazine.

In truth, few people in the industry have had so meteoric a rise to fame and fortune as Ben has.

At the still young age of 44, he runs a growing industrial empire as Chairman of the Board of Diversified Metals Corp., which recently changed its name to Diversified Industries, Inc., to reflect the new business activities of a company that began as a non-ferrous metals dealer.

Direct to the point as always, Ben says confidently: "Diversified's growth is only beginning. I'm shooting for a billion dollars in sales within a few years and I know our organization can accomplish this."

(Diversified's sales for the fiscal year ended last October were almost $250 million versus $150 million the year before, while total assets rose to $104 million from $60 million.)

Ben, who once traveled five states in a 2-ton pickup truck hunting scrap 16 to 18 back-breaking hours a day, is now hunting instead for more quality acquisitions to add to the growing Diversified family.

And when Ben picked the name Diversified in 1956, he apparently was looking far into the future for no other word could have proved more appropriate.

Diversified is now truly diversified.

The company has been split into four divisions: Metals and Industrial, Automotive and Transportation, Consumer, and Advanced Technology and Service.

Belonging to the various divisions of Diversified Industries are such quality companies as Diversified Metals, Scullin Steel, Duro Pen, Kimco Auto Products, Liberty Smelting Works (1962) Ltd., Pioneer Synthetics, Diversified Dismantling, Consumer Home Products, Diversified Metals International, American Leisure Products, Middlewest Freightways, Metals Supply Service, The George Sall Metals Co., Western Non-Ferrous Metals, United Refining & Smelting, Nathan S. Colen & Son, Creative Metals, Wilpet Tool & Manufacturing, and even an insurance agency—Diversified Underwriters.

Is Diversified a conglomerate?

"Absolutely not," Ben insists. "We have made all of our acquisitions in a sensible, complementary manner. In a word, they mesh. They were not picked off at random just to add on sales. We have looked for top management, growth and profitability in making all of our acquisitions."

Ben, who describes himself as "an alley-wise street fighter"—a reference to his youth spent in the tough Kerry Patch section of St. Louis—still drives as hard, and perhaps harder, than he did at the beginning of his business career. His constant companion is a telephone, which he uses in making deals from his office, his home, while breakfasting at one of several St. Louis restaurants, and even at the Jewish Community Center, where he regularly plays handball and jogs several miles early every morning.

But it was not always this way.

For if there ever was a man who was NOT "Born to the Purple," as the expression goes, it was Ben Fixman.

As a boy he sold newspapers and worked as a janitor. He was forced to drop out of high school after only eight months to support his mother since his father had died while he was an infant.

In 1947—at the age of 22—he left a women's ready-to-wear chain —at the time he was managing 13 units—to go into the scrap business.

"I had an almost insatiable desire to be in business for myself," he recalls. But a recession plummeted scrap metal prices in 1949 and he was forced to the sidelines. For a brief time he operated a landscaping business and even sold baby chairs door-to-door before re-entering the scrap metals business later in 1949. Finally in 1951, he opened his first scrap yard in St. Louis.

Ben has always been an innovator, an "idea man." "I remember coming out with the first brochure for the scrap metal business. It had colored photographs and it gave the industry a touch of class."

In 1954, Ben and Irv Fischer, a life-time friend, formed Fischer-Fixman Metals Co. Two years later Ben bought his partner out and changed the name to Diversified Metals. (Incidentally, Irv's young son, Ken, now directs one of DMC's West Coast operations.)

In the early 1960's, there came a vital point in the fortunes of Diversified.

After much experimentation, frustration and hard work, Ben and Leo M. Paradoski, now president of Diversified's Metals Division, developed the famous "Cold Process" for reclaiming copper and aluminum wire mechanically from its binding insulations.

The "Cold Process," as opposed to the industry's traditional burning method, gave the scrap industry a new image and helped set the stage for Diversified's take-off to success.

In March of 1966, Diversified went public, selling its initial offering at $9 a share. Since then the stock went at one point to $110, taking into consideration a stock split.

As has been stated, Ben is little changed by all this financial success.

He is still regarded as "one of the boys" by his friends, and if you are a friend his loyalty knows no bounds. But if anyone ever tried to cross him in a business deal it turns out that Ben has a long, long memory.

Outside of Diversified, Ben has two main interests: his family, which includes his lovely wife Marilyn and their three daughters, one of whom has presented Ben with a beautiful granddaughter. That is interest number one.

His second interest has been in philanthropic endeavors, particularly in fund-raising for the State of Israel, which he has visited many times. To help Jews in need, Ben has given grandly of his time and his money.

Upon reflecting, it would seem that although Diversified has branched into myriad fields and is no longer strictly a metals company, Ben's greatest pleasure is still to get on that phone and make a profitable deal.

"I love it," he often shouts—for all the office to hear—after having concluded one.

United States Senate
WASHINGTON, D.C. 20510

December 10, 1970

Mr. Ben Fixman
9914 Litzsinger
St. Louis, Missouri

Dear Ben:

This is just a note to tell you how much I enjoyed meeting you and your wife at the Brandeis Club reception and dinner.

Lou Sussman has told me many times what a great group you have in St. Louis, and I certainly must agree -- it was a most pleasant evening for me.

If your travels should bring you to Washington and if you have a moment, do drop by the office to say "hello".

In the meantime, my best wishes for the coming year.

Sincerely,

Senator Ted Kennedy was kind enough to write me a note inviting me to drop by his office when I was in Washington.

Through my philanthropic work, I met many interesting and powerful people. To my left is Senator Ted Kennedy of Massachusetts, "The Lion of the Senate," and on my right is my dear friend, Morris Lefton, one of the nation's leading experts in the field of aluminum.

president; the enterprising scrap man who became a corporate executive and founded an industrial empire."

The story noted that I had founded the Marilyn Fixman Cancer Center at Jewish Hospital in memory of my beloved wife Marilyn, who died in 1980. It also mentioned that I had donated $250,000 to establish Camp Sabra, a camp for children in the Missouri Ozarks. (How I wish someone had established a summer camp for me when I was a dirt-poor kid in the Carr Street ghetto.)

Camp Sabra

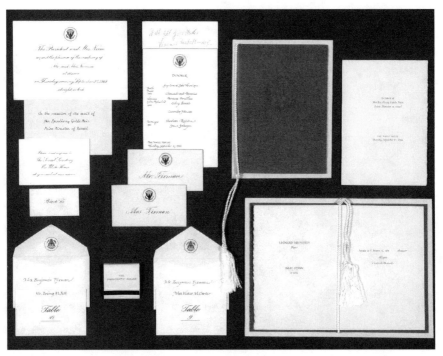

Invitation, program and other printed pieces for the Golda Meir State Dinner.

The story continued: "This is a man who cannot remember turning down any charitable appeal; a man who has given to such diverse causes as the Jesuit Living and Learning Program, the American Italian Earthquake Appeal, the Anti-Drug Abuse Educational Fund, the United Way, the National Jewish Hospital/National Asthma Center, organizations helping the mentally retarded, and poor people who couldn't pay their utility bills."

The story described me as a "fearless industrialist and feisty flag waver who has a spine of steel, a velvet heart, the guts of Superman, the business brains of a tycoon and the spunk of an entrepreneur."

The *Globe* story was published at the very same time as Diversified's anti-trust suit was being heard by the jury. I am fully convinced that the

Marilyn and I attended a State Dinner at the White House honoring Prime Minister Golda Meir, Israel's "Iron Lady." The dinner was hosted by President Nixon.

story helped immensely in portraying me in a very favorable light and contributed to our eventual victory in the courtroom.

But of all the honors and recognition I received in my career, the one that held a special significance for me was being named "Man of the Century" by *Scrap Age* magazine, the leading publication in our industry. I was really pumped up by this story because it meant recognition from my peers over my contributions to the metals industry in America.

Marilyn and I—with a little help from Max Fisher—received an invitation to attend a State Dinner at the White House held in honor of Golda Meir. Richard Nixon—the man who famously said, "Your President is not a crook," (he was lying, of course)—was the host of the Meir dinner, which was a fabulous affair.

The second White House dinner I attended was for the Shah of Iran when Jimmy Carter was President. I took my daughter Jody because by this time Marilyn was far too ill to travel. I never liked Carter from the beginning and his outrageous statements concerning the State of Israel confirmed my belief that he was an anti-Semite. Carter also admitted in a *Playboy* magazine article that he had a sexual "lust in my heart."

This only furthered my belief that besides being an anti-Semite, he was also *meshuga*. What kind of man, especially a President of the United States, would admit to the American public and the world that he was guilty of having a little lust in his heart? Lust is O.K., but keep it to yourself. CU

CHAPTER NINE
THE JEW AND THE JAP

All of us can remember a day that changed our lives forever. For me that day came late in the 1960s when my phone rang at home.

"Ben," Martin Zalk, my friend, said. "I've got a guy you've just got to meet. He's wonderful. You'll just love him. I know it. He's your kind of man."

After this kind of build-up, I was intrigued. So I said to Zalk, "Bring him right over."

Ten minutes later, my doorbell rings and in comes Zalk accompanied by a tall, handsome, immaculately dressed Jap named Shig Katayama.

That meeting turned into a 45-year "love affair" as Shig and I hit it off immediately and eventually became "closer than brothers." The foundation for our relationship was built around our mutual respect for each other and the fact that we both felt "our word was our bond." Shig and I did multi-million-dollar business deals on the basis of just a handshake between us. No lawyers, no contracts, no bullshit. Everything we did together was out in the open—strictly aboveboard.

Reader's Digest magazine used to run a column entitled: "The Most Unforgettable Character I've Ever Met." For me, that person was Shig.

His family (wife, Hanna, and daughters, Tracy and Nancy) and my family (Marilyn and my daughters, Janis, Barbara and Jody) regularly attended weddings, *bar mitzvahs,* and all family gatherings together.

Shig, who was born in Los Angeles, was a highly successful business entrepreneur, a huge gambler (horses, Las Vegas craps and pro football), but most of all a charitable and excellent family man. He also happened to possess the foulest mouth I have ever heard from any human being on the planet earth.

A typical sentence from Shig would run something like this: "Fuck you, fuck me, fuck her, fuck thee." Followed by "fuck it all."

My wife, Marilyn, once told him: "Shig, I'm going to take a bar of soap and wash out your mouth." But nothing could change Shig. Profanity streamed from his mouth like the torrent of water endlessly going over Niagara Falls. Shig never stopped using the f-word, and he didn't care where he was or who happened to be listening to him.

Besides being business entrepreneurs, Shig and I had one other interest in common: gambling. We spent many nights together at the crap tables at the Dunes Casino in Las Vegas. Shig was an absolute madman when he held the dice. He made huge bets, and if the dice were "ice cold," he could easily drop $25,000 in just a few minutes. It didn't matter to him. He just loved the action, and so did I. In Vegas I was known at the Dunes as "Mr. F" while Shig was known as "Mr. K." In truth, we both should have been known as "Mr. D"—as in dumbbell because between us we probably dropped enough millions to have built our very own casino. Occasionally, the dice would run "hot" and we would walk away as big winners. But we were both smart enough to know that once you went to the tables, the casinos owned you. They had the odds in their favor and that "edge" was always working against the players, no matter what the game: craps, roulette, the slots or poker. But who really cared? Action was the name of the game.

And speaking of the Dunes, around 1970, I received an offer to buy the Dunes Hotel and Casino from the principal shareholders, Sid Wyman, Bob Rice and Charlie Rich. What they were asking for the property was $16 million in the form of a convertible debenture from my company,

Diversified Industries. The U. S. Government had indicted all three men and they were naturally worried about their futures. (By the way, all three were eventually exonerated.)

When I told Marilyn I had a chance to buy the Dunes, my wife, who was so desperately ill with cancer, pleaded with me not to get involved with "those people." So I promised her that I would reject their offer. Marilyn might have thought that if I owned the Dunes, I might stray and get involved with a showgirl, but there was no chance of that because I loved Marilyn with all my heart and soul.

A long-time friend that I grew up with, Steve Lekometros, a well-known St. Louis bookmaker and former hat presser, also warned me against buying the Dunes. "Forget about it, Benny," Steve implored me. "Stay away from those people. We're dear friends, but if you do this deal, I will have your legs broken. You don't know what in hell you are getting into."

But getting back to Shig, the real love of his life were racehorses. At one time, Shig owned 64 horses. (Can you imagine the monthly training and the vet bills for 64 thoroughbreds?) He ran them at tracks like Santa Anita, Hollywood Park and Golden Gate. His stable of horses ranged from moderate claiming price animals to stakes horses.

> BY THE WAY, YEARS LATER WHEN THE DUNES WAS FINALLY SOLD, THE SELLING PRICE WAS $150 MILLION, A FAR CRY FROM THE $16 MILLION I COULD HAVE HAD THE PROPERTY FOR. OH WELL, WIN SOME, LOSE SOME.

Shig insisted on going first class in whatever he did, and horse racing was no different. He didn't want any young "Mickey Mouse" jocks screwing up his horses and so he insisted on only the best riders like Hall of Famers Lafitt Pincay and Braulio Baeza—the Babe Ruth and Lou Gehrig of the sport. (By the way, the best definition of horse

The Jap and the Jew: The true "Odd Couple,"
we were like brothers for more than 45 years.

racing that I have ever heard was: "Horse racing is the 'Sport of Kings' played by paupers.")

Shig liked to motivate his jockeys and before a race began, he would slip into their riding boots a considerable sum of "win" tickets to make certain the jocks would give him their best effort and collect "a little something extra" for themselves. Shig believed money was a great motivator of people—and he was right.

I'll never forget the night Shig and I went to a small racetrack, Cahokia Downs, located near East St. Louis, Ill., a track which ultimately went kaput. Shig was extremely unhappy and frowning as soon as we entered the track. "This is the ugliest, most broken-down track I have ever seen," he complained to me. "On a scale of one to ten, it's not even a one."

He wanted to leave, but I talked him into staying and we went into the dining room to watch the races from a glass-enclosed setting.

The first race was about to start. "Who do you like, Fixman?" I told him I liked the odds-on favorite, whose price was 3-5. "O.K.," Shig said, "I'm going to bet $5,000 to win on him."

"Shig," I said, "you must be insane. If you put $5,000 on that horse, you'll end up betting against yourself. You can't make $5,000 bets at this track. They just can't handle that kind of action. This is basically a track for small bettors, people who bet $5 and $10 a race."

"Fixman [he always called me by my last name], what kind of piss-ant track did you take me to? Shit, I can't even make a lousy little $5,000 bet." We stayed for a few more races and then we hit the road. End of the evening.

But Shig really didn't have to worry about winning money at the gaming tables because he was a first-rate entrepreneur who became involved in multiple business deals over the span of his lifetime. Sometimes he lost money because he thought that all the people he became involved with were honest, trustworthy, and well-intentioned like him. Con artists were always trying to get involved in deals with Shig because they knew he had money and always trusted people.

But by and large, Shig did very well in the business world. As an example, when an associate reneged on a gambling debt, Shig acquired the man's business, a small vending machine company, in settlement of the debt. Shig took that tiny company and built it into the largest vending machine company in all of Japan, and in the 1990s, he sold that company for $300 million.

Shig also purchased the franchise rights for the Western United States for a so-called "burn bed" to be used in hospitals to help patients who had been horribly burned. The "beaded burn bed" was a great invention, but there was one drawback—hospitals could not afford the $34,000 cost. Consequently, at first sales were sluggish. But that all changed when Shig's company president, Dr. Wally Weil, a professor of business from the University of Wisconsin, came up with the idea of leasing, not selling, the beds to hospitals. The leasing idea turned the trick,

> EARLY ON, SHIG HAD OFFERED ME A 50 PERCENT "PIECE OF THE ACTION" IN THE "BURN BED" FRANCHISE AT A COST OF JUST $250,000, BUT SINCE I WAS THE CEO OF A PUBLICLY HELD COMPANY, I DID NOT WANT TO GET INVOLVED IN ANY SIDE DEALS. SO I PASSED ON THE DEAL, WHICH ETHICALLY WAS THE RIGHT THING TO DO.

and hospitals quickly came on board. Shig later sold that franchise for $37 million.

One bad business deal cost Shig more than $10 million. He got involved with "an ivory tower-type" professor who had an idea for a super high-power microscope for use in the medical field. Shig invested his millions with the professor who eventually manufactured the microscope. It did everything the professor said it would do. But like many people who live in an "ivory tower," the professor didn't have any common sense or "street smarts." The microscope worked, but its selling price was beyond astronomical. No one could afford it. I told Shig to learn from the experience and not to get involved with "degreed idiots" who didn't understand the realities of the business world. Stick with people who have street smarts, I said, and he agreed.

Shig and I grew closer and closer as the years passed. I even became his "bookie," and every Sunday he would bet 14 NFL games and I would "take his action," a $1,000 bet on each game. He usually lost and I told him: "Shig, you can't beat the NFL games. It's impossible over a long season. The 'vig' will just eat you up."

"Fixman," Shig shot back at me, "I don't give a shit. It gives me something to do on Sundays."

In 1993, Shig and I went into business in a big way. We formed Kataman Metals, with headquarters based in St. Louis. Kataman (partly named for each of us) quickly established itself as a leading international supplier of copper, aluminum and zinc. I ran the day-to-day operations of the company, while Shig maintained his usual role of "the money man." Shig never interfered once in the daily operations of the company. He knew I was more than capable of handling the buying and selling of materials and he would rather be with his family or else spending the afternoons watching his horses perform at Santa Anita, where he was a highly recognizable patron of the ponies.

Many years before, like the brothers we were, we gave each other our word that whichever one of us outlived the other, the survivor would deliver the eulogy for the one who had passed away.

Sadly, that day arrived in 2007. True to my word, I headed to Los Angeles to give the eulogy for Shig. I was in a wheelchair, recovering from painful knee surgery, and I had to have the assistance of my daughters, Jody and Barbara, to get to the West Coast. CU

Here is the eulogy I delivered for Shig:

"I am Ben Fixman. For those of you who do not know me, I have had the privilege of being Shig's business partner and close personal friend for some 45 years. I am here before you today to fulfill a promise Shig and I made to each other years ago when we were young, strong and eager to take on the challenges life brought.

Back then, because of the mutual respect we had for each other and our close personal relationship, we gave each other our word that whichever one of us outlived the other, the survivor would give the eulogy for the one who passed away.

So to Nancy, Tracy, Sang and the rest of Shig's family and his friends who gather here today, I stand here sadly to say a few words about my dearest friend, Shig Katayama.

Each of us has seen the grave marker of a family member or friend who has passed away. We notice the date of birth and the date of death, but we usually pay little attention to the dash that separates those two dates.

To me, it is not the birth date representing the beginning of life that is important. Nor is it the date of death, the ending of this life, that should be given special notice. Rather, what deserves recognition is that small dash that separates those dates.

That dash represents the time we spent on this earth. It encompasses all the hopes and dreams of our loved one and friend. Within that span are all our successes and failures, all our joys and sadnesses. It encompasses our family, the friends we make along life's path and the reputation or legacy we leave behind.

Each of us has his or her memory of Shig, all of which encompass his dash or life. I ask that each of you spend some time recalling your life's adventures with Shig and the wonderful memories he has left with you.

I would like to take a few moments to pass along some of my memories and experiences with Shig.

Shig and I were introduced to each other by a mutual friend, Mort Zalk, some 45 years ago. Mort told me, 'Ben, when you meet this guy, you will fall in love with him.' Those words were prophetic as Shig and I loved each other as brothers from virtually the day we met.

Over the years, that relationship grew from one of personal respect and admiration to one that was extremely personal between our families. We celebrated together at each other's joyous events—weddings, births, grandchildren and business successes.

But we were also there for each other during very trying times—the death of a spouse, business difficulties, and other challenges that life brings. We were great sounding boards to each other and we bounced ideas off one another, but we never forced our views on the other.

Shortly after Shig and I met, I took my wife, Marilyn, to meet Shig and his family. My wife was impressed with Shig's beautiful daughters, Tracy and Nancy, and the lovely hospitality she received from Shig's wife, Hanna. Shortly after our meeting, we traveled to Japan where Shig became our tour guide, showing us all the wonderful sights of his ancestral country.

On the trip, I wanted to purchase some expensive pearls and other jewelry for my wife and daughters, but found I had spent most of my cash on the trip. Without hesitation, Shig wrote his own large check to pay for the items even though our friendship was still very young and a solid relationship had not yet been cemented.

Needless to say, I immediately repaid Shig when I returned home, but that's the kind of man Shig was—trusting—sometimes to a fault. But if you were Shig's friend, he was always reliable, trustworthy and there for you. I hope in some small way I reciprocated in kind for Shig and his family.

People have asked me how it was that two people of such different *heritages could be so close. On the surface, one would not expect Shig, with his Japanese heritage and Asian customs, to be close friends with me, a person from Midwest America, with a European, Jewish background.*

As unlikely as it may seem, the relationship worked. I believe it worked in large part because of Shig's belief in the underlying goodness of people. Shig trusted people. He treated people with dignity and respect. He taught me that the measure of a person was not what they had of a material nature, but rather what was in a person's heart. It is a profound lesson that Shig taught me—one, which I hope I have been able to follow in my life.

Shig opened a new world for me in another area as well—horse racing. Because of Shig's love for horses, I also got deeply involved in horse racing. Shig encouraged me to become an owner of horses. Thinking Shig had never steered me wrong, I took his advice and bought a few horses that I raced on the East Coast.

It was one of my worst business decisions, one that I still regret. Shig loved every aspect of horse racing and horse breeding. He used to tell me: 'Ben, maybe you shouldn't own something that eats and ...' Well, you know what else. I would tell him: 'Shig, you can win a race, but you can't beat racing.' But horse racing was Shig's passion and he would never listen.

You know, there was another thing besides my experience with horse racing that Shig was responsible for—my vocabulary of swear words increased immeasurably.

Over the years, our personal relationship transformed into a business relationship. That relationship was based on trust and loyalty. In the relationship between Shig and me, our word was our bond. If one of us said something, the other knew he could rely on it.

As a result, being the entrepreneur that he was, it didn't take Shig long to get into the non-ferrous metals business in Japan, and we began doing millions of dollars of business together on a handshake basis.

From there, Shig and I engaged in joint venturing steel that happened to be in short supply at the time. Shig used his numerous contacts in Japan to source the steel and I handled the selling. Shig was highly thought of in Japan and his reputation opened many doors for him. We also joint ventured in a project to sell Japanese steel-making technology in the United States.

About this time, Shig was having some difficulties in Japan and asked for my help in accompanying him before the Japanese Diet. I offered my support and he accepted without hesitation. When this problem was ultimately resolved in his favor, Shig used an expression 'Gidi' to show his appreciation. He said it means, 'I owe you.' I told him, 'Shig, I only did for you what you would have done for me. We are like brothers.'

In 1994, I wanted to retire and sell my company to a group of foreign investors, in part because of some financial difficulties the company was experiencing. Shig encouraged me not to sell and offered me whatever I needed financially. Despite the offer, I nevertheless sold my interest in the business and retired—at least temporarily.

Shig's generosity to a friend was overwhelming. I loved that about Shig and I would like to think I have learned from his example of loyalty. But to those of us who had the privilege of knowing Shig, we recognize that's just the type of person he was.

My retirement was short-lived. I knew Shig always loved new business opportunities. It didn't matter whether it was vending machines, hospital beds, microscopes, steel companies, tour companies, loan companies or real estate. It didn't matter. If Shig thought there was a potential to building something, he was interested.

So 14 years ago, Shig and I became partners in a metals trading business. Shig and I would communicate nearly every day about markets, opportunities, operations, everything involving a business. We were also partners in a telecommunications business, which he later turned over to Nancy and Tracy.

Both businesses were highly successful. Shig was the type of businessman that gave complete trust and responsibility to his managers. It was an expression of Shig's underlying faith and trust in others. Some times it did not work out for the best, but that was Shig's personality and who he was.

I could go on for hours talking about Shig, but it is time for others to think about their own personal relationship with a truly inspiring, generous, trusting and loyal individual. I wish that it were not up to me to be the one standing here today.

It is I—no, it is we who are here today—who are indebted to you for all you have provided, for the lessons you have taught us and for the cherished way of life you have shown us.

To my brother, may you rest in peace and I hope with all my heart that one day we will be together again.

My dear friend, sayonara."

CHAPTER TEN

I EASILY WIN A PROXY FIGHT, SAVE MY FAMILY IN A KIDNAP THREAT, LOSE SOME VALUABLE PAINTINGS TO AN ART THIEF, AND GET BADLY BURNED IN A POSH RESTAURANT

In 1971, I acquired a small St. Louis area company that wasn't doing very well. I brought its owner to Diversified as a vice president because I had been told this person was a very competent executive.

Around this time, Diversified was encountering problems with its bank loans, its subsidiaries were in a business slump, and, worst of all, my wife Marilyn's breast cancer was becoming more aggressive.

Needless to say, this combination of negative events brought me to the brink of depression and in April of 1972, I stepped down as president of Diversified but retained the title of chairman.

I put in as president the man whose company I had acquired in 1971. This man, who I thought was my friend, immediately turned against me. He started a campaign of trying to influence the board of directors (to which he had added three of his allies) against me, with the ultimate goal of ousting me from the company of which I was its largest shareholder and its most knowledgeable "metals man."

This man, who really did not understand the basic workings of our Metals Division—traditionally, the biggest moneymaker within Diversified—wanted to go in other business directions.

When I heard that this man was trying to undermine me with the board, I, of course, felt upset and disappointed at this lack of loyalty. But I held my peace and did not intervene because as the largest shareholder, I wanted to see the company do well. I even went along with him when he asked me to move to another office building in Clayton. I was doing the best I could to promote harmony.

Then another upsetting event occurred. This man reneged on a salary agreement reached between himself and Morris Lefton, who had asked for higher compensation to run Diversified's Metals Group. Lefton, in my opinion, was absolutely entitled to higher compensation because he was a huge asset to Diversified based on his expertise in metals, particularly in the aluminum field, where he was held in high esteem by his peers. Denied what he rightly had coming to him, Lefton left Diversified and formed his own trading company, which turned into an extremely huge and successful enterprise.

The loss of Lefton further upset me, but the crowning blow came when this man came up with the idea of going to our banks and asking them for a "haircut," a reduction in the amount of money Diversified owed them on loans totaling $47 million.

I objected vehemently to the idea of asking the banks for a "haircut." The banks had lent money to Diversified in good faith, and it would have been unethical to not repay that money in full.

That's a lesson I had learned as a kid in the ghetto. When I bought a loaf of bread for 10 cents on credit, the grocer was always repaid as soon as we had the money. Ten cents or $47 million—it didn't matter because the principle was the same: You always repaid your debts in full.

By now, I was thoroughly disenchanted—and thoroughly aggravated —by this man's actions and his dismissive attitude toward me.

I had had enough. It was time to take back my company. So in March of 1974, with the help of a friend and ally, Jerry Castle, I initiated a proxy fight to regain the company I had founded.

Some proxy fights can go on forever, but not this one. It was an early T.K.O. It was all over in just about three months as I captured 78.7 percent of the votes and ousted the man who had turned on me. And I saw to it that the banks were repaid their $47 million in loans down to the very last penny.

In the interest of fairness, I must say that the man I defeated in the proxy fight went on to build a very large and profitable company.

He did have talent as a business executive, but because of his actions at Diversified, he was a person that I never would have anything to do with again. To this day—almost 35 years later—I have never spoken to this man.

As a newspaper reporter once wrote about me: "If Ben is your friend, he is your friend for life. But if you ever try to cross him, he has a long memory." Truer words were never spoken.

MY FAMILY BECOMES THE TARGET
OF A ROBBERY AND KIDNAPPING

Sometimes having money and being in the public eye can combine to form a dangerous, lethal combination. It almost did for the Fixman family in the late 1960s.

This terror arose shortly after I had cashed in $9.5 million in a secondary offering of Diversified's stock.

Just after I took down the $9.5 million, rumors from highly reliable inside sources reached me indicating that I was being set up for a home robbery and the theft of expensive jewelry. Then I was told that the robbery threat had escalated into a plan to kidnap one of my children.

I was told the threat came from "known St. Louis underworld figures with a past history of multiple violent crimes."

But no one was going to victimize my family—not if I could help it.

The first thing I did was to evacuate my cancer-stricken wife Marilyn and our three daughters, Janis, Barbara and Jody, to a place of safety. I took them to nearby Temple Israel where I knew they would be out of harm's way.

Once they were safe inside the Temple, a 12-man police unit—commanded by my close friend, the chief of detectives for St. Louis County—moved into my home awaiting the intruders. They were all heavily armed, as we expected a "bloodbath." I also carried a weapon, as did a close friend of mine.

The police stayed in my home for 26 straight hours, but the threat never materialized, thank God.

But I had had enough of seeing my family and myself frightened out of our minds and fearful for our lives.

I decided to make one phone call and that action literally saved the day for the Fixman family.

I called my good friend, Morris Shenker, the famed criminal defense attorney who knew all the major players in the St. Louis Mafia.

I told Morris of my problem and he immediately arranged a sit-down with the man who allegedly was the kingpin of the Mafia in our city.

He came right to the point. "Ben," he said, "I know of you and I know that you are a good man with a good reputation who financially helps out all kinds of people who are down and out. I'll take care of this kidnapping problem myself, and there will be no further problems.

"Please go home and tell your wonderful wife and daughters that they will always be safe."

I knew that what this man said was "the law among his followers" and I offered him $50,000 as a payment for his protection. He refused to take even one single penny from me, and from that day forward the robbery-kidnap threat never came up again and my family lived in peace.

In the decade of the 1970s, St. Louis had the reputation of being "the bomb capital of the country" because of many fatal car bombings instigated by rival gangsters. One day in July of 1970, I was at work in my office in the Pierre Laclede building in suburban Clayton when I heard a tremendous explosion. Phillip Lucier, the head of Continental Telephone Corporation and the father of 11 children, was killed as he backed his car out of the building's outdoor parking lot. Newspaper reports said the bomb went off when Lucier turned on the car's ignition.

Needless to say, I was a bit unnerved by the proximity of the bomb since my car was parked not too far from Lucier's. The next day the FBI went through the building, interviewing people and seeking information. I was one of those people the FBI interviewed. The crime was never solved and remains a mystery some 40 years later. The effect the incident had on me? I found a different parking place deep within the building. Why take chances?

THE CASE OF THE MISSING PAINTINGS: WHO TOOK MY LEROY NEIMANS?

In 1978, an extremely good friend of mine—who shall remain nameless—told me he had the shorts. Translation: He was running low on money.

I was more than glad to help him out and wrote him a check for $100,000. I didn't want it, but he absolutely insisted on giving me as collateral on the loan three large (6- by 4-foot) original oil paintings by LeRoy Neiman that hung on his office walls. (See plates 5 and 6) The paintings were of St. Louis Blues hockey players in a game action, plus action in a polo game.

I told my friend to keep the paintings and let them remain in his office. I never brought the subject up again. Five years passed, and in 1983, he asked me to take the three paintings in satisfaction of the $100,000 loan. I agreed.

*I married Elaine (Cookie) Blumoff in 1985. Cookie has been
a wonderful companion for all of our marriage.*

I was never an art connoisseur by any means (they don't teach art appreciation courses in the ghetto), but I had always liked Neiman's work, particularly the way he used vivid colors to blur the action of sporting events.

In fact, I liked his work so much that I brought three more of his paintings (for the total sum of $34,500) that had previously hung in the St. Louis Playboy Club before it folded its doors and set all of those beautiful, buxom Bunnies free from hustling drinks and occasionally hustling themselves.

I now owned six Neimans at a total cost of $134,500. I had the whole lot appraised and insured the paintings for $350,000. Little did I know it then, but that was some good thinking on my part.

I hung the three Playboy paintings in the lower level of my home. When I remarried in 1985, my new wife, Cookie, and I decided our home was just too damn large for two people. So we sold our house to baseball Hall-of-Famer Ozzie Smith and we moved into a high-rise condo. But there was just not enough room in our new home for the massive Neiman paintings so I decided to put them up for sale.

I chanced to be in Los Angeles on a business trip and learned that the well-respected Lawrence Ross Art Gallery on Rodeo Drive in Beverly Hills was planning a major showing of Neiman art and was taking pieces on consignment.

Everyone I talked to told me the Ross Gallery had an impeccable reputation, so I shipped all six paintings to the gallery. (It turned out later there was a moral to this story: Don't believe everything you hear.)

Over the next several months, I asked Rick Beldner, Diversified's general counsel, to call the gallery owner and see if any of the paintings had been purchased. Every time Rick called, he got the same answer: "No sales yet. It's probably because hockey isn't a big sport in California."

Finally, after eight months of fruitless calls, I decided enough was enough and I wrote the Ross Gallery requesting the return of my Neimans. Dead-ass silence was their response. By luck, we finally caught up with Lawrence Ross one day. He said the gallery had gone out of business and was, in fact, in bankruptcy proceedings. Then he hung up the phone.

I was not about to be fucked with, so I asked a friend of mine who lived in L.A., Eddie Schulman, to go to the gallery and see if the Neimans were still there. Eddie visited the gallery, then he called me: "Benny, someone went south with the Neimans. There isn't one left in the whole damn gallery. You've been *yentsed* (swindled)."

I then dispatched Rick Beldner to L.A. to "find out what in the hell was going on." When Rick went to the gallery, he was told that Lawrence Ross was no longer employed there. Ross was in an unknown place and so were my paintings.

We immediately filed a theft report with the Beverly Hills Police Department. Rick's detective work uncovered the fact that two weeks before the gallery closed, a Neiman painting called the "Music Man" had been shipped to a Mr. Bill Mack, who lived in Minneapolis.

We contacted Mr. Mack and found out that he was an artist who had sent his own property to the Ross Gallery. But when the gallery couldn't pay him, they negotiated a settlement under which he accepted the "Music Man" in exchange for what he was owed.

Mack later blew his stack when he learned the "Music Man" was not the property of the gallery, but he made a deal with the insurance company, paying them a certain amount of money so he could keep the "Music Man."

As for me, I came out real well. The insurance company paid me $350,000 for my loss—not a bad return on an investment of $134,500.

To this day (late 2009), the other five Neiman paintings have never been found. They just up and vanished like a fart in the wind.

■ ■ ■

The Neiman incident was not the first time in my life that someone I trusted turned out to be a *momzer* (a cheating bastard).

When I put my home up for sale, Ozzie Smith told me that I should deal with his agent in negotiating a price for my home.

One day I got a call from the agent who, in addition to being a consultant to famous athletes, also happened to train horses. He and I met several times and then I got the idea that I might facilitate the sale of my home more quickly if I had some sort of business arrangement with the agent.

So I told him to buy me a horse, train it and race it in California. Pretty soon I was the owner of an animal, and I began receiving large training bills every month. When I called the trainer and asked him when the horse was going to actually run, I was told: "His legs are sore. He'll have to heal up first. If we run him now, it might ruin him for life." What did I know about horses? Nothing. So I accepted the trainer's word that the horse wasn't ready to be entered in a race.

This went on for months. All I got were more training and vet bills and the same refrain from the trainer: "The horse is still sore."

Finally, my patience was gone. I put in a call to the trainer to tell him that I intended to get rid of both him and the horse but, lo and behold, they were both gone to places unknown.

I enlisted a private investigator to solve the mystery of the missing trainer and horse and here is what he reported back to me: "The trainer took your horse to Mexico, changed its name and has been running races regularly. In fact, he won several races and took down substantial purse money." (Of course, I never saw one penny of the winnings.)

Shortly after that the trainer and my horse dropped out of sight—vanished once again like that proverbial fart in the wind.

I GET BURNED BADLY—TWICE

Every Friday night without fail, two longtime friends, Dick Cutter and Al Hoffman, and I would have dinner together in the fabulous Tenderloin Room at the Chase Hotel.

On one such Friday, we decided to order cherries jubilee for dessert. The restaurant normally used Sterno in preparing this dish, but they had run out of Sterno and some numbskull substituted alcohol to prepare the flaming dish. When the waiter ignited the alcohol, it shot a steam of fire onto my face. Agony, pure agony ensued. Cutter kicked over the table, yanked off the tablecloth and tried to wrap it around my face while I was trying to protect my face with my hands.

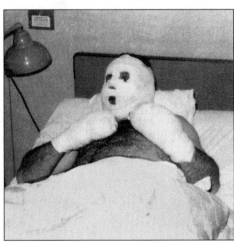

Here I am in a bed at Jewish Hospital. When I look at this photo years later, I can almost smile. But when I remember the horrific pain caused by those burns, that smile quickly disappears. I will always be eternally grateful to Dick Cutter and Al Hoffman for rescuing me from the flames. Dick is still with us but, unfortunately, Al has passed on.

They rushed me to nearby Jewish Hospital where they immediately began to treat me for second and third degree burns of my face and hands. The pain was beyond excruciating. They kept me in the hospital for two weeks. Luckily, I found a great St. Louis plastic surgeon, Dr. Jim Chamness, who in eight different surgical procedures, removed the excess skin so there would be no scars left from this terrible incident. And in a wonderful application of his skills as a surgeon, Dr. Chamness did exactly that.

What I needed next was a top-notch legal mind, and so I retained Mortimer Rosecan, who had just settled a case for $165,000 and had the reputation of being one of the top trial lawyers in the City of St. Louis.

Rosecan spoke with the insurance company and told me they were offering me $15,000 and would go no higher. He said he thought it was a fair offer and that I should accept the $15,000. I couldn't believe it. Fifteen thousand for all the pain and agony I had gone through—plus the fact that my out-of-pocket medical expenses were $25,000 GREATER than the $15,000 I was being offered.

Very reluctantly, I accepted the $15,000, but I should have held out for more. Much more. So you could say that I got burned twice, once at the restaurant, and once by some poor legal advice.

I learned an indelible lesson from that restaurant fire: "Don't always rely on your lawyer as the final word. It can't hurt to use your own good judgment."

PEOPLE DO THE CRAZIEST THINGS

Over my years as a businessman, I somehow came into contact with people whose behavior bordered on the bizarre. Here are a few examples:

■ ■ ■

When it came time to pay his income taxes, one of our middle management financial people challenged the IRS, claiming the U.S. dollar was not the true standard for conducting transactions. Accordingly, he filed a return—claiming a huge loss—based upon a completely irrational "Gold Standard" formula that he had dreamed up. Of course, the IRS went berserk and was on his case in a New York minute. Claiming tax fraud, the IRS put extreme pressure on this man. And, of course, he eventually paid the government his tax obligation. I could have told him that he had a better chance of flapping his arms and flying to Mars than beating the IRS.

■ ■ ■

Then there was the executive who ran our Dismantling Division. This company owned a house in Bal Harbour, Florida. I chanced to be in that city one day on a business trip when I saw a sign at the entrance to the city that stated: "NO JEWS ALLOWED." I told the executive to get rid of the house immediately and he did exactly that, which suggested that he was a sensitive, rational person.

Not too long after that this same married man and his secret girlfriend were flying in a small plane he was piloting over Tennessee. The plane struck a mountain and both of them were killed instantly. So much for acting rationally.

■ ■ ■

I have saved "the weirdest person I ever met" for the very last. He was an employee who wrote his memos to me in Yiddish because he knew I was Jewish and thought I would be impressed. In the middle of our anti-trust suit against AT&T, this person would put on a jogging suit and run around the federal courthouse every day, praying that an attorney would subpoena him to testify. However, neither side would call him because they knew he was so dangerously unstable. One night at 3 a.m., I got a call at home from the police telling me that they had caught an intruder in my metals processing plant. The intruder was bare-ass naked and was running around the plant floor kicking a huge helium balloon he had tied to his penis. Immediately, I knew who it was and told the cops: "He's harmless. Just give him a ride home."

THE AVA STEEL EXPERIENCE

When I stepped down as president of Diversified, I no longer had the day-to-day responsibilities of managing the company. Instead, I now had the freedom to explore other business opportunities. One opportunity that immediately peaked my interest was getting into the steel business.

At the time—1972—steel was in short supply because the federal government had imposed restrictions on importing foreign steel. Without the competition from cheap, foreign steel, the government was helping to protect domestic steelmakers by enabling them to keep the price of domestically produced steel high. Anyone who had a source of domestic material had no trouble selling it at a large profit because of the shortage created by government regulations. I had an opportunity because I had a source.

A friend of mine, Jerry Castle, was chairman of the board of Penn-Dixie Corporation and Penn-Dixie owned a company called Continental Steel. Among other things, Continental Steel made steel wire rod, a widely used product with many applications, including use in manufacturing such products as fencing and coat hangers. I approached Castle to find out what it would take to buy steel from Continental. Castle proposed that if I would commit to taking a substantial quantity of steel wire rod at a fixed price over an extended period of time, Continental would sell it to me.

This represented a huge financial obligation so before committing, I wanted to make sure I had the proper sales people in place to sell the steel. After an extensive search, I hired a gentleman named Sherman Wolfson and set up an office in New York City, which we staffed to handle the selling effort. With the personnel in place, I contacted Castle and agreed to his terms. Thus, AVA Steel Products was born, and I was now the proud owner of an enormous quantity of wire rod. I was hopeful—and confident—I could sell it.

I was often asked where the name AVA came from. It is the first letter of the names of my first three grandchildren: Amy, Valarie and Adam.

I've never been one who wanted to be subject to the risks of rising or falling metals prices. To protect against this risk and to lock in the profit on this metal, AVA entered into long-term supply contracts with customers at fixed prices. Wire rod was in such short supply at the time that customers would plead with us to increase their allocation, but we could only sell what we had. The arrangement worked like a charm. Metal would go from Continental to our customers and the bucks— BIG BUCKS—rolled into AVA. We never touched the metal. No trucks, no warehouses, no yard, no equipment, and no employees (other than selling and administrative staff). Just profit!

The most rewarding outcome of getting into the steel business was to afford me the opportunity to get into my first business relationship with Shig. I had met Shig a few years before and we had kept in touch with each other. I knew Shig had experience in the steel business and had a number of relationships with companies in the Far East that manufactured steel. Shig was keenly interested in what I was doing with AVA Steel and we kept looking for ways we could combine his Far East connections with AVA's United States customer base. Finally, the right opportunity presented itself.

Shig had a close relationship with a Japanese trading company named Asahi Bussan. The trading company had, in turn, fostered a relationship with a relatively new Japanese steel manufacturer named Azuma Steel. As a relative newcomer, Azuma was looking for access to the American market and was willing to sell at a very competitive price to get it. Because the material could be brought into this country within the quantity limitations agreed upon between Japan and the United States, a genuine opportunity for AVA existed. I was invited to Japan and after several meetings, a business relationship was finalized. AVA became the exclusive marketer of Azuma Steel wire rod in the United States. We paid Shig and Asahi Bussan a commission on every pound of wire rod purchased. The relationship worked beautifully for everyone. Most important, our customers were ecstatic because we offered them a product in short supply at a very attractive price. They were eager to enter into a two-year contract with us and we were only too happy to oblige. The timing was perfect because our contract with Continental Steel was running out and we could not count on them as a continuing source.

Everything went along fine for many months, but in business, there are no guarantees and nothing lasts forever. The economy slipped and there was suddenly an abundance of steel at cheap prices. Our customers wanted price concessions and threatened to renege on their contracts. I was absolutely confident our contract would be upheld if it came to litigation, but that would not have been in anyone's interest at that time. So we went to every customer and offered to reduce the price if the customer would agree to increase the quantity they were purchasing from AVA and extend their contract for an additional year. Everyone accepted the proposal. All the relationships and anticipated profits continued for an extra year.

There was an even more unique opportunity that came to AVA from the relationship with Shig and Asahi Bussan, but unfortunately that one did not turn out as we had hoped. Had it worked out, the profits would have been enormous.

Shig informed me the management of Asahi Bussan had a relationship with Toshin Steel. Toshin had a patented technology that enabled them to make steel in a fraction of the time it took American steelmakers. The essence of the technology was to use an oxygen lance to super heat the furnace. To accomplish this, the furnace was lined with a special ceramic brick. Special water jackets were strategically placed in the ceramic lining to cool the bricks. The ability to use a hotter, temperature-reduced melt time, resulted in less labor and a substantially cheaper cost to make steel.

Shig and I saw an opportunity to sell this technology to American steel makers but neither of us had sufficient expertise in making steel to know whether the process was as advertised. We learned one of the foremost authorities on making steel in the United States was a Father William Hogan. He was associated with Fordham University. We met with Father Hogan and sought his advice. After a generous contribution to the university through the good father, he agreed to accompany us to Japan to witness the technology in operation and to provide technical advice.

The technology was everything it was advertised to be. We were all duly impressed with what we saw and Father Hogan could not have been more enthusiastic. Shig and I began thinking about how we would bring the technology to America and revolutionize our antiquated steel industry. It's probably also fair to say we were both seeing dollar signs. To handle the task of selling the technology, we hired Robert Lubker, a gentleman who was familiar with the industry. We made several trips to Tokyo and after months of discussion, a joint venture was formed known as AVA-Toshin Service and Supply Co.

Lubker went to work and in no time at all, made a sale to United States Steel. It was agreed that the technology would be tried first on a single furnace to see how it worked and if successful, equipment for additional furnaces would be ordered. The engineering was completed, the ceramic bricks and water jackets arrived and were installed, water lines were put in and the testing began. Everything worked like a charm. The engineers at U.S. Steel could hardly contain themselves when they saw how fast the steel was produced—AND THAT'S WHEN THE PROBLEM STARTED. Despite the success of the trial, no further orders were forthcoming. We spoke to the engineers and to management but nobody would give us a straight answer. Finally Lubker got wind on the Q.T. of what had happened. The test had been too successful. When union representatives learned what had transpired, they feared the loss of union jobs. We were told, though we were never able to verify it, that the union threatened to strike if the new technology was implemented and jobs were lost. The incentive of reduced costs had vanished and with it all our dreams of revolutionizing the steel industry. Of course, the dollar signs disappeared as well.

As for AVA Steel, that business had also run its course. In March 1980, the "Trigger Price System" the federal government had imposed to protect American steel makers from foreign "dumping" was lifted and the restrictions on bringing foreign steel into the United States ended. Steel became plentiful and prices dropped. Our customers could now go directly to steel producers who were only too willing to sell direct. AVA's role as a middleman with a source of supply vanished, as did the profit potential. If that were not enough, there was now another activity to which I had to devote nearly all my time. By this time, I had regained control of Diversified and was deeply involved in the anti-trust litigation against AT&T, which was commenced in 1978. But AVA was a great run. I was fortunate enough to meet and work with some truly wonderful people.

AND WHAT A MISSED OPPORTUNITY THAT WAS! IF THE UNION HAD NOT DERAILED OUR GAME PLAN, PROFITS WOULD HAVE BEEN BEYOND BELIEF. THERE WOULD NOT HAVE BEEN A CALCULATOR IN EXISTENCE WITH ENOUGH ZEROES ON IT TO FIGURE OUT HOW MUCH MONEY WE WOULD HAVE MADE. CU

CHAPTER ELEVEN
MENTSCHEN
Stanley Abel and Stanley Yarmuth

Mentschen, used to describe people of integrity and humanity, is the highest compliment in Yiddish.

During my lifetime, I have had the privilege of meeting several people who fit the description of a *mentsch*.

The first *mentsch*—a man I have known for more than 40 years—is a dapper, articulate, highly intelligent New Yorker who has made his living on Wall Street. His name is Stanley Abel and shortly after I met Stanley I dubbed him "The Magician of Wall Street." Why? Because when he was an account executive at Lehman Brothers, Stanley had the uncanny knack of finding lesser-known companies whose stock was ready to take off to the moon.

"Ben always regarded me as an alchemist, a man who could take certain companies and turn them into gold," Stanley said. "As for our personal relationship, it couldn't be closer. I regard Ben as one of the most loyal persons I have ever known. He is also one of the most optimistic persons I have ever met. One of the greatest joys in his life is doing for his friends."

Stanley and I first met at a meeting of security analysts in the late 1960's in New York City. "Ben was talking about the merits of Diversified and I chanced to ask him a non-too-bright question from the floor. He quickly replied that he was happy that I had asked that question. His response was so supportive of me that it triggered an immediate affinity between us.

The dapper Stanley Abel

"Ben and I were birds of a feather. We both shot straight from the shoulder. We told it the way it was and we both had a deep and abiding belief that Wall Street was crammed full of con artists and hustlers looking to separate good people from their hard-earned money."

I credit Stanley for laying on me the nickname of "The Throbber," in recognition of the warm feelings for people that emanate from my heart—along with my penchant for opening my purse for humane causes.

I also credit Stanley with introducing me to Ruth Axe, who was head of the highly successful Axe-Houghton Mutual Fund. That fund purchased a substantial portion—somewhere around 3.5 million shares—of my common stock when I did a $9.5 million secondary offering in 1967.

My wife, Cookie, and I remained close to the Abels over the years. When Stanley and his wife, Mary, went on their honeymoon to Paris in 1987, we accompanied them. We all stayed at the Ritz and had one hell of a time. One highlight was dining at Maxim's, a world-famous restaurant that was 116 years old. Someone told me that years earlier, Communist leader Ho Chi Minh had worked there as a busboy. Big deal, I thought, no one remembered me for having been a janitor in St. Louis.

In 1975, Stanley co-founded Abel/Noser, a Wall Street firm of institutional discount brokers that is prospering despite the bleak national economy. Abel/Noser, whose accounts run into the thousands, services clients such as Harvard University, Shriners Hospital for Crippled Children, New York City Retirement Systems, Florida Power and Light, Goodyear Tire, Avon—and on and on.

I was still ravenously hungry after they fed us on the Concorde, so I deliberately faked "grabbing 40 winks" but kept my mouth wide open so the stewardess might slide another piece of tasty fish on top of my tongue. Across the aisle, Stanley and Mary Abel enjoyed my antics. They didn't know I'll do anything for food.

Who says British food is not the best? Not us. Here we are at the Horse and Groom Pub in Windsor shoveling down the food as if it were going out of style. My wife, Cookie, second from the left, showed the greatest restraint of any of us. She had a normal meal.

British Guardsmen wearing their traditional bearskin hats provided us with a magnificent moment when we were in London.

Mary and Stanley share a contemplative moment standing on a bridge in Vienna. Helping Mary and Stanley celebrate their marriage and tagging along with them on their honeymoon gave us indelible moments Cookie and I will never forget. We also visited the French Riviera and greatly enjoyed Cannes, Nice and Monte Carlo. All in all, a truly wonderful trip.

Stanley is 77 years old now, still goes to work every single day and, like the U.S. Marines, is "looking for a few good men" (or women) for his organization.

STANLEY YARMUTH

Stanley Yarmuth, who made his fortune in Louisville, Kentucky, as the founder of National Industries, a large conglomerate, was a *mentsch* in every sense of the word.

A self-made businessman who started out in the auto business, Stanley was uncommonly smart, unwaveringly honest and absolutely true to his word. He was the hardest-working person I have ever known and he possessed a kind heart for the unfortunate of the world.

But above all else, Stanley was an excellent family man who was devoted to his wife, Edna, and their three sons, John, William and Bob, who all pursued and achieved notably successful careers.

I first met Stanley in 1966 in New York City, around the time I had taken my company public. To say we hit it off immediately would be an understatement. In a short period of time, we became close buddies, chatting on the phone with each other almost every day of the week.

Stanley and I were born four months apart the same year, 1925.

Stanley Yarmuth

As the older of the two, I thought I had "ribbing rights." And so I constantly kidded him about the fact that the only reason he was smarter than I was stemmed from the fact that he had attended three years of college at New York University, while I was a graduate of the School of Hard Knocks, located in the Carr Street ghetto in St. Louis.

If Stanley saw a business opportunity in an operation that he thought was not maximizing its profit potential, he went right after it. That's why he made a bid to purchase the world-famous Churchill Downs racetrack. He never was able to acquire that property, but his proposed acquisition of the track was a solid indicator of his fearlessness and daring in the world of business.

Stanley had his eye on a property that my company owned. It was St. Louis-based Middlewest Freightways, and I agreed to sell it to him. A new president was installed at the truck line. His name was Marvin Cherry, one of my dearest lifelong friends whom I first met more than 70 years ago. (That's right—70 years.)

Marvin had absolutely no knowledge of the trucking industry, having been an executive in the *shmateh* (clothing) business. But he did possess the most important asset of all: street smarts. In just a few years under Marvin's direction, the truck line's sales soared from $20 million to $100 million annually. I knew Marvin was the right man for the job and his performance exceeded even my own expectations.

Then one day—out of the blue—Stanley Yarmuth called me with terrible news. He had been diagnosed with a super-aggressive type of cancer. Very quickly, Stanley began chemotherapy. I would fly to Louisville and take him to the hospital for some of his chemo treatments. But they didn't help and Stanley passed away on Sept. 15, 1975. He was just 50 years old. I was a pallbearer at his funeral and I felt it was an honor to have been asked to perform that duty on behalf of my dear friend.

Whoever said, "The good die young" certainly had Stanley in mind.

In retrospect, the good genes and good works of Stanley and Edna Yarmuth were passed on to their three sons for, as they say, "The apples don't fall far from the tree."

John Yarmuth, a Democrat, became Kentucky's first Jewish Congressman. As giving as his father, John donated his post-tax 2007 Congressional salary of $120,000 to charities in Louisville. He was re-elected in 2008 with 59 percent of the vote.

William Yarmuth is president-ceo of Almost Family, Inc., one of the nation's largest providers of home healthcare services. Founded in 1985 in Louisville, the company last reported annual sales of more than $130 million and has over 5,500 employees. It is a publicly traded company.

Bob Yarmuth is president of Sonny's Real Pit Bar-B-Q, a chain of restaurants located throughout the southwestern United States. Sonny's recently celebrated its 40th anniversary—and in honor of that anniversary, made a substantial monetary commitment to the March of Dimes.

In 1987, the University of Louisville Yarmuth Book Award program was established. Initially, 53 schools were part of the program. Over the years, it has grown substantially to include more and more schools across the state of Kentucky plus schools in southern Indiana.

The purpose of the program is to recognize deserving high school juniors "who show academic promise, intellectual achievement and who are community-service oriented."

The program is funded by an endowment from the family of John Yarmuth to honor his father, Stanley, who gave his family "one of the greatest gifts of all—the desire to learn." CU

CHAPTER TWELVE

YOU CAN'T KEEP AN OLD WARHORSE DOWN
THE WILD DECADE OF THE 1990s:

A Bad Baron Causes a Bankruptcy,
Kataman Metals is Created,
I enter the Restaurant Business—and
Eat Everything in Sight,
This Jewish Man Performs a Priestly Miracle
A Little Needling from my Daughters

In 1991, I was 66 years old and it was time to think about a well-earned retirement. I had enough money to last me three lifetimes and I looked forward to not being involved in the daily grind of the business world—to just kicking back and enjoying the rest of my life in the so-called "Golden Years." (Whom was I kidding?)

And, in 1991, an Austrian baron and a group of his investors approached me about taking control of Diversified Industries. An executive in Diversified's Metals Group had introduced me to the baron.

On paper, the match and timing seemed perfect. Naturally, I wouldn't make a move before I had investigators check out the baron. All of their reports were glowing. The vetting of the baron revealed that he was an extremely wealthy individual who had extensive real estate holdings in Austria and the United States, plus a good-sized interest in a brewery.

More importantly, the baron owned a publication called *Brook Hunt*, a trade journal regarded as the authoritative publication for the metals industry worldwide. The investigators reported that the baron was on a first-name basis with some of the most well-known chief executive officers throughout the metals industry.

I thought to myself: What an impressive resumé this man had.

During our financial negotiations, the baron stressed that if a deal was struck between us, he would bring substantial new investment monies into Diversified. He would also "take out" Diversified's existing bank lenders and replace the bankers by providing his own sources of financing, which he said would greatly enhance Diversified's future.

I was satisfied—as were my advisers—that the baron was the man we were looking for. So, in September of 1991, I sold a portion of my stock to him and turned over the control of the company to him. I resigned as chairman of Diversified Industries and headed into retirement.

Or so I thought.

Right after taking control of Diversified, the real baron showed up—unsavory and cunning with a high-handed attitude that offended everyone. He immediately alienated Diversified's bank lenders by threatening them with being replaced if they did not provide more favorable lending terms. In an arrogant manner, he told the banks that he had his own investors plus international banks ready to step in and kick the banks out if the terms of Diversified's loans were not amended.

Banks do not like being played "hard ball" with and as the months passed by, it became clear that the baron had neither additional investors nor other banks that would commit funding to the company. Furthermore, when pressed, the baron refused to use any more of his own cash to fund Diversified. In essence, the baron intended to use OPM (other people's money) to make his scheme work.

The baron was a bluffer and the banks were about to call his losing hand. Irritated by the bluster and false promises of the baron and his management team, the bank demanded that the "other lenders" the baron always spoke of be brought in immediately to take out the lending institutions.

And to put even more pressure on the baron, the banks continued to severely restrict cash available for business operations, which forced the liquidation of Diversified's assets to pay down their loans.

With his bluff called and with no sources of further financing available, the baron—the so-called blue-blooded aristocrat who loved to boast to the entire world how moral and truthful a person he was—put Diversified into a bankruptcy filing in March of 1993.

I was so furious at the baron that I could hardly control myself. If he and I had been in the same room, only one of us would have emerged—and that would have been the kid from the ghetto. Legally, there was not a thing I could have done to prevent the bankruptcy filing. I was helpless because I was just a director at the time, serving on the board the baron had packed with his ass-kissing friends who helped him destroy Diversified and bring about hard times for its employees, stockholders and creditors.

The corporation I had worked decades to build was

THERE IS AN INTERESTING SIDE STORY THAT FURTHER ILLUSTRATES THE BARON'S TRUE CHARACTER. A CLOSE FRIEND OF MINE, ST. LOUIS BUSINESSMAN JOE SIMPKINS, INVESTED $250,000 WITH THE BARON TO HELP SECURE FINANCING FOR DIVERSIFIED. WHEN THE TIME CAME FOR THE BARON TO HONOR THE "PUT" CLAUSE IN THE AGREEMENT, HE REFUSED TO REPAY JOE HIS MONEY. I WAS INFURIATED AND STEPPED IN PERSONALLY. IN THE MEANTIME, JOE UNFORTUNATELY PASSED AWAY. BUT I CONTINUED TO PRESS FOR TWO JUDGMENTS AGAINST THE BARON'S ASSETS. WHEN I GOT THE SECOND JUDGMENT ON THE BARON'S ASSETS IN ENGLAND, HE FINALLY REPAID THE $250,000, EVERY PENNY OF WHICH WENT TO JOE'S FAMILY. I DIDN'T CARE HOW MUCH IT COST ME; I WAS NOT ABOUT TO LET A DEAR FRIEND OF MINE GET TAKEN BY AN ARISTOCRATIC CON ARTIST.

now down in the shitter—all because of one man's lies and greed, a man who masqueraded behind an aristocratic title, boastful resumes, half-truths and promises you could wipe your ass with.

But, truth be told, the reorganization of Diversified was a boon for me personally. The cliché of turning lemons into lemonade became a reality.

How?

As part of the reorganization, Diversified was forced to terminate the activities of its Diversified Metals, Inc. trading operations. That's when Shig Katayama—who was my partner—and I formed Kataman Metals, Inc. in June of 1993, just two months after the bankruptcy filing.

KATAMAN|K
METALS

We hired the entire workforce of executives and personnel who had worked for Diversified Metals. And what a highly talented team of experienced and successful metal traders these people were!

It was like starting a new business with only All-Stars at the core of your company.

New banks were brought in to fund Kataman and the company was extremely profitable from the first month it opened its doors to the day of its sale in late 2007. Once Kataman went into action, I was back in action—doing what I did best, trading metals. My retirement was short-lived but, as my life story shows, I'm not the shy, retiring type.

■ ■ ■

But good times never seem to last, especially in the world of business. The sale of Kataman Metals became necessary after Shig was stricken with cancer. Of course, the first thing he wanted to do was to provide financial security for his family.

By this time, Kataman was extremely well-established and highly respected throughout the industry, and we desired to pass the torch to a new ownership group that would be fully committed to making the company continue to grow and maintain its tradition of excellence.

Two major companies approached us, but we rejected both of them because they did not seem to be a "good fit" with Kataman.

But the third group that approached Kataman was absolutely perfect. It consisted of David Blue, a major investor; chief executive officer Joe Reinmann; and chief financial officer Robert Gieryn. Under their leadership, Kataman has continued its pattern of growth and has become an even stronger player within the industry.

All three executives have tons of experience in the metals industry. They are highly intelligent, aggressive, innovative, and they are committed to working long, long hours to get the job done properly.

Along with president Warren Gelman and executive vice president John DePetro Jr., they constitute a premier team of industry professionals who provide a solid foundation that insures Kataman's continued success in the future.

On a personal note, I want to thank the new owners for the courtesies and respect they have shown toward me on a daily basis. I would like them to know how much I appreciate their efforts in making me feel right at home over the past few years.

Shig and I could not have sold out to a finer group of gentlemen.

In retrospect , I was proud of my role in making Kataman grow so quickly and so successfully.

In 2006, the last full year that Shig and I owned Kataman, sales climbed to $873 million and they continued to skyrocket. At the time Shig and I sold the company, sales for calendar 2007 were solidly on track to bust the billion-dollar mark.

I ENTER THE COMMUNICATIONS BUSINESS

Kataman Metals, Inc. was certified as a minority-owned business as a result of the Japanese ancestry of my partner, Shig Katayama. Because of this, I had the opportunity to meet an individual named James Webb, who was the executive director of the St. Louis Minority Business Council. Jim was an extremely bright and respected former executive for what was then Southwestern Bell Telephone. Jim's position with the St. Louis Minority Business Council allowed him to become aware that Kataman Metals sold a lot of copper to wire and cable manufacturers. He believed many of the telephone companies would be interested in buying wire and cable through a minority-owned company. I've never been one to let an opportunity pass and Jim's suggestion of forming a business to sell copper or wire to the telephone companies seemed to have a lot of merit. I was particularly intrigued with the idea because I had spent years servicing the telephone industry while running Diversified Metals. After a few discussions, Webb, Shig and I agreed to form Kataman Communications, LLC, in late 1996 with Webb serving as president.

> THROUGHOUT MY BUSINESS CAREER, I ALWAYS HAD A KNACK FOR SPOTTING PEOPLE WHO WOULD PROVE TO BE TALENTED EXECUTIVES. WHEN I FIRST MET JIM WEBB, I KNEW INSTANTLY HE WOULD BECOME A VERY VALUABLE ASSET TO KATAMAN COMMUNICATIONS—AND MY JUDGMENT OF HIM PROVED TO BE CORRECT.

Our initial enthusiasm for the business model began to fade after about a year when it became clear the telephone companies we were soliciting already had long-term supply contracts in place with major wire and cable manufacturers. We simply were unable to break into the existing supply chains. We determined we would have to look for other opportunities to make a buck.

Webb became aware that certain contracts for telephone service at facilities owned by the City of St. Louis required the participation of a minority-owned business. Using Webb's contacts at Southwestern Bell, we entered into a subcontract agreement under which Kataman Communications participated with Southwestern Bell to provide telephone service at Lambert-St. Louis International Airport. Later we also participated with Southwestern Bell in providing telephone service to inmates at the St. Louis City Jail. We purchased, installed and maintained the equipment, and Kataman Communications became quite successful. We used the experience we gained to get similar contracts at other airports.

The success we initially experienced lasted for several years, but then circumstances beyond our control began to have a rather rapid, negative impact on our revenue and profits. The first blow was the sudden explosion in the use of cell phones. As the proliferation of these devices increased, fewer and fewer travelers found it necessary to use the coin phones installed at the airports. Today, virtually everyone has a cell phone and coin-operated telephones are becoming an ancient relic. The second major blow was the September 11, 2001, terrorist attack. Following the attack, only passengers were allowed through security into the gate area. Individuals who were waiting for the arrival of passengers could no longer wait at the gate, and that is where the majority of the telephones had been installed. The inability of people to get to the phones resulted in a further reduction of our revenue. By the time the contract to provide this service ended, our revenue generated at airports had dropped to virtually nothing.

During this period, however, another opportunity presented itself. The contract to operate telephones for the State of Missouri prison system was put out for bid. The bid specification required that 20 percent of the revenue be allocated to firms certified as a minority-business enterprises. Kataman Communications had such a certification as a result of the minority status of Webb and Shig. Because of our prior experience operating public telephones at airports and in serving inmates at city- and county-operated jails, we offered to participate as the minority business partner with MCI, the current telephone service provider. Ultimately, MCI was the successful bidder and we went forward as its minority business partner. To handle our part of the project, the inmate telephone systems at three state prisons were assigned to Kataman Communications to operate. Our role under the contract lasted for approximately seven years. At that time, the contract expired and a new contract was submitted to the public for bid.

By this time, Webb had left Kataman Communications due to health reasons and he ultimately returned to his prior position as head of the St. Louis Minority Business Council. In addition, Shig had been diagnosed with cancer and he had far more serious concerns on his mind. Shig and I were now in our 80s and neither of us needed the money. The fire and the drive for the success of this enterprise no longer seemed important under these circumstances. We had started Kataman Communications more as a challenge than anything else. Perhaps Shig and I just needed to prove to ourselves that the two old warhorses still had what it takes to build a profitable business from scratch. Shig and I discussed what we wanted to do and we came to the conclusion to simply wind up the affairs of the company upon the expiration of all existing contracts.

In looking back, the venture was very successful; however, it was important to realize that a business does not last forever. Kataman Communications' life cycle had run its course. I believe one of the most important things I took away from this experience was the friendship I made and have kept with Jim Webb. In addition, after watching Shig's cancer progress and cause the ultimate death of my dearest friend, I knew pursuing monetary rewards was not the most important thing in life. My experience with Kataman Communications proved to be a learning experience that was fulfilling and rewarding on many different levels. But the time had come to shut it down and move to other things.

IF YOU WANT TO FEED YOUR FACE, BIG BAD BENNY'S IS THE PERFECT PLACE

At the same time I was dealing with that rascal, the baron, two friends whom I had financed in the restaurant business were having *tsores* (big trouble) in making a go of it. Putting it bluntly, the restaurant was dying.

I said to myself, if I once ran a $330 million in sales NYSE company, then I certainly could revive a failing Italian restaurant located in a shopping center in St. Louis County. It would be a piece of cake and I could feed my face to my heart's content.

Owning a restaurant had always been a secret desire of mine. I liked the idea of being the official taster of all the dishes that came out of the kitchen and of being a half-ass cook. The idea also appealed to me because it would be a perfect place to have a good *kibitz* (to socialize aimlessly) with all of my friends.

So I put my heart and soul—and unfortunately, my mouth—into turning around the restaurant, which was beautifully furnished with tasteful art and a huge collection of Tiffany lamps. But art and lamps don't sell food. So I upgraded and expanded our menu, changed cooks and hired young and attractive waitresses and waiters who were on the ball and eager to make a buck.

In quick order, the restaurant began to take off and Big Bad Benny's was the place to go. In fact, the food was now so outstanding that I couldn't get enough of it and I quickly gained 25 pounds. (Try getting that much weight off on a treadmill! To do it, you would have to run from St. Louis to Singapore.)

In short order, the restaurant received two rave notices in the *St. Louis Post-Dispatch*. Joe Pollack, the paper's excellent restaurant reviewer, praised our chili to the sky and Jerry Berger, the paper's gossip columnist who was read by absolutely everyone in St. Louis, said our barbecue was out of this world.

These stories, naturally, created a boom in our business and since I was a born promoter, I told my public relations man, Don Roth, to write an advertising column in the shopping center's monthly throwaway paper. I told Don I wanted some really outrageous stuff in the column, the crazier the stories the better.

Here are two examples of the wild stories we ran:

"Pardon us for interrupting your sleep the other morning at 4 a.m., but the big bang you heard was caused by one of our chartered planes air-dropping a huge load of freshly caught Atlantic cod onto our parking lot. That's how we can offer you the freshest fish in town."

And...

BULLETIN

"We are sorry to report that one of our chartered planes—flying over Europe with a cargo of caviar—strayed into Russian air space and was shot down by a Soviet missile, killing the crew and eliminating caviar from our menu. But please don't forget our great ribs, huge steaks, palate-pleasing pastas, fabulous chili and the best in St. Louis barbecue."

Despite our great food, our business began to slide. Patrons were just not coming into the restaurant like they used to, which frustrated me until I figured out the reason. Actually, there were three reasons and they were all the same: location, location, location.

BBB's was tucked away—and almost partly hidden—in a tiny corner of an immense shopping center. We were not permitted to put up any advertising signs on the street that bordered the shopping center, nor on Olive Boulevard, a major thoroughfare about a block away from BBB's that carried tens of thousands of vehicles daily.

Our poor location was killing us. But now there arose an even greater problem—with our landlord. A very large Italian restaurant had moved into the shopping center and naturally they regarded us as competition and wanted to see us gone.

There was no doubt in my mind that this new restaurant put pressure on the landlord to try to oust us from the shopping center. Much earlier, the four representatives of the landlord and I had shaken hands in agreeing to a new lease for BBB's. Then one day I got a phone call from one of the four leasing representatives saying they needed to go over the lease again. I knew this phone call could mean only one thing: trouble—and I was right. They asked for a meeting and I said come over to the restaurant right now. All my life, when trouble loomed, I believed in facing problems head-on and in an immediate manner.

The four of them wasted no time. They said that although we had shaken hands on a new lease, they now wanted to insert a stipulation that the landlord had the legal right to approve BBB's menu.

My reaction was instant and right to the point: "Go fuck yourselves." I got so angry that I challenged each of the four *goyim* to step outside onto the parking lot where I would be pleased "to kick the shit out of each of you."

At this time, I was in my late 60s—and I might have ended up on the losing side but I didn't give a damn. We had shaken hands on a deal and they had reneged. I felt as if I was back in the ghetto and spoiling for a fight. Damn the consequences.

But, as I expected, the men all backed off from this crazy, insane Jew who wanted to take all of them on. What the four men didn't know was that I always carried a pair of brass knuckles with me "just in case of a tie" and that I always had a loaded .38 revolver nearby—also, "just in case of a tie." Growing up in the ghetto amidst a criminal element had taught me one thing: how to be prepared if trouble came my way.

Shortly after my run-in with my reneging landlord, my days as a restaurant owner came to a close. I shut the doors and auctioned off everything at BBB's. Out of business. Finito. Gone.

But I had learned a valuable lesson: location, location, location—and it was wonderful to be able to lose some weight since my days as a food taster were now history.

I GO TO LUNCH AND SAVE A LIFE

One summer's day in 1990, I was standing in the cafeteria line waiting my turn to be served at Garavelli's, an extremely popular restaurant then located on Manchester Road in west St. Louis County.

It was noon and, as usual, the place was packed. The line of customers snaked outside of the entrance door and spilled onto the parking lot. The scores of people didn't mind waiting because Garavelli's food was great, the portions were huge and the prices were very affordable. Besides, the customers loved to exchange small talk with the owner, my dear friend, Steve Lekemetros.

I was just about to give the sandwich maker my order when I heard a series of screams. I looked over the dining room and saw a priest in a wheelchair, sitting at a table with two nuns. The priest was in deep trouble. Food had lodged in his throat, cutting off his airway and his ability to breathe. He was turning blue.

The hundreds of restaurant patrons all froze. Not one of them made a move to save the priest's life. Not one.

Someone has to help this priest, I thought—and that someone was yours truly. I bolted from the serving line and ran to the priest who was turning bluer right before my eyes. I put my arms around him and yanked him out of his

wheelchair. (Although I was 65 years old when this happened, I still possessed the arms of a *shtarkeit* (strong person) from all those years of lifting and moving metals.)

I clamped my arms around the priest's abdomen and squeezed him as hard as I could. Suddenly, large particles of food were forcefully ejected from his throat and mouth and his breathing quickly returned to normal. An ambulance took the priest to a hospital for a check-up and he was discharged hours later.

The incident received coverage in the local media and several days later I received a thank you note from the priest, a member of the clergy of Saint Nicholas Greek Orthodox Church, one of the larger Greek Orthodox churches in the Midwest.

Several people at the restaurant asked me where I had learned the Heimlich maneuver, which saved the priest's life. They all wanted to know if I had received formal training in the Heimlich. "No," I replied, "I once saw somebody do it in a movie." And that's the honest truth.

In reflecting on the whole incident, I thought to myself, "When I was 12 years old, I struck a rabbi in Hebrew School because he rapped my knuckles with a ruler. Now, 53 years later, I helped to save the life of a priest who was in distress. God, it took me more than five decades to square things. Now, we're all even."

A LITTLE NEEDLING FROM MY DAUGHTERS

When my three *tochters* (daughters) Janis, Barbara and Jody, heard that a book was being written about their father, they naturally chimed in with some thoughts of their own on my outrageous lifestyle. They kidded me about what the Jews call *oyska fafen a gelt*, which means throwing money away.

My daughters put their heads together and came up with a list of how—in their minds—I spent money in an excessive fashion. Frankly, I enjoyed the needling they gave their father.

They gave me a good ribbing for:
- Buying condos in Florida.
- Every so often, providing call girls for company customers.
- Owning multiple swimming pools and hot tubs.
- Driving expensive cars like Mercedes, BMWs and Cadillacs.
- Giving some "big bread" to fund presidential campaigns.
- Purchasing top-of-the-line Brioni suits and buying tons of custom-made shirts, all featuring the finest Egyptian cotton.
- Installing a handball court and a Dairy Queen machine in my home, plus a massive cedar closet fit for a king.
- Buying some really expensive pieces of art.
- Regularly flying to Las Vegas and using only high denomination chips at the crap tables.
- And, finally, paying outrageous fees to lawyers.

I may have been guilty of a few financial excesses in my life, but as I told my three precious daughters: "When I finally close my eyes, you, your children and your grandchildren will not have a financial care in the world."

I may have played fast and loose with some big bucks during my lifetime, but when it came to my beloved family, I never forgot that a good father must always be a good provider for those he truly loves.

LOUIS B. SUSMAN

As I have said, there were many executives who worked for Diversified Industries and then moved on to unbelievable recognition and success later in their careers.

One outstanding example is Louis B. Susman who was selected by President Barack Obama to be the United States Ambassador to the United Kingdom, one of the most coveted and powerful ambassadorships in the world.

Susman, who at one time was Diversified's general counsel, was confirmed to his new position by the United States Senate on July 10, 2009.

Lou, whom I have known for decades, is following in the footsteps of such famous Americans who later became U.S. Presidents: John Adams and his son, John Quincy Adams, James Monroe, Martin Van Buren and James Buchanan.

The list would eventually include such noted personages as Andrew W. Mellon, Joseph P. Kennedy, Sr., W. Averell Harriman and Walter Annenberg.

I personally wish Lou every success in his new diplomatic undertaking, and I know he will perform admirably and be a source of pride to all Americans. CU

CHAPTER THIRTEEN
LIKE THE SONG SAID: "I DID IT MY WAY"

I'm 84 years old as this book is written, and I realize that time is definitely not on my side. I have been a realist all of my life and I know that no man is immortal. So I am ready to accept the inevitable.

Frankly, I wish I was 18 years old again and dead-ass broke. I'd like nothing better than to start all over because I truly believe I could duplicate my life story—of going from a ghetto kid's dream to the reality of business success after promising myself I would never be dirt poor again. I made that promise at age 7, while shivering in the bitter cold on a downtown St Louis street corner peddling newspapers in the Depression year of 1932.

There are certain people in this world who are "survivors." These are people who triumph in life despite the often long odds against them. Their determination to succeed is so powerful that it blows away all obstacles in their path. "Survivor" is a tag that I believe could easily be pinned on me.

The philosopher, Henry David Thoreau, said: "The mass of men lead lives of quiet desperation." I think that is true, but not in my case. I never went along with the crowd. I had my own set of values and principles. I truly danced to the tune of a different drummer, and I outlived every single person I grew up with in that ghastly ghetto. That's what the value of hard work will do for a person. I worked so hard and such long hours in growing my metals business that my employees nicknamed me "The White Tornado."

The greatest joy in my life naturally has come from my family: my magnificent wife, Marilyn, who God took away from me at a very early age, and our three daughters, Janis, Barbara and Jody, who have all grown into compassionate, caring and loving adults. My three "babies" remain—and always will be—the true loves of my life, as are my five grandchildren and seven great-grandchildren. When push comes to shove in this world, your family is all that really matters. Family comes before anything else on this earth. Money, fame and recognition—they are nothing and all fade away with time. But family is forever.

One thing I learned early in my business career is that you can't do it alone. You must build your company with dedicated people. And you've got to be good to these people by keeping your word to them and letting them "make a taste." I used to tell my employees: "Look, first take care of the company. Then if there's any room left, take care of yourselves." That was all right with me because many of them were going to do it any way. Many of the people who worked for me at Diversified Metals became millionaires. I gave them extremely low-priced options, and our stock skyrocketed from its opening price of $9 a share to the equivalent of $132. Good for them; they deserved it. And I felt good about it, too, because I knew it was a godsend to my employees and their children.

All my life I have tried to help people who had helped me. When I lived in the ghetto, a neighbor named Lillian Corson used to eat barbecue ribs and then give me the bare bones to suck on after she was finished. And I was glad to get those bones. They were a real treat. Decades later, Lillian's mother, Rose, was in a nursing home. Gradually her health failed her, and she needed costly around-the-clock nurses, which Lillian absolutely could not afford. So I picked up Rose's entire tab. I never forget a favor, but if someone tried to shaft me, they got paid back in spades.

In all my memories of the ghetto, my mother, Rose, was of course the central and dominating figure. She was the glue that held us together. Without her, the Fixman family absolutely would have perished. Rose taught all of us the value of keeping your word, of paying your debts, of being ethical and of being good religious Jews. She worked for one measly dollar a day, cleaning homes so her five children could have some food to eat. She ate whatever food remained after her children had eaten—and the pickings were always slim. She subsisted on toasted rye and schmaltz (chicken fat). She ate that same meal of toasted rye and schmaltz every day that we lived in the ghetto.

One day, at the age of 89, she told me: "My son, I have lived my life. I don't want to live anymore." And then she was gone.

■ ■ ■

My days at age 84 are typically divided between a little business (being retired is really a bitch because I miss the action of making a deal) and a little pleasure (playing small-stakes gin rummy with close friends).

In the mornings, I go to Kataman Metals for a few hours where I am a consultant to the company that I and Shig Katayama (The Jew and The Jap) founded. It is a real pleasure to go to Kataman. The executives, metals traders and secretaries are all highly intelligent, hard working and very down-to-earth. All in all, they are a great group to be associated with. I eagerly look forward to being in their presence every day.

After leaving Kataman, I drive to the Men's Health Club of the Jewish Community Center for an afternoon of passing time by playing gin rummy.

The Men's Health Club, to which I have belonged for decades, is made up mainly of old Jews who just sit around and basically "shoot the shit." The most ancient of the members know their time is coming, and they are just trying to squeeze out a few more precious years. Their conversation is hysterical and loaded with curses: "You putz, you schmuck, you dickhead." Those are some of the more common

The new Jewish Community Center in St. Louis

expressions that fill the air.

Thank God, a new and magnificent Jewish Community Center opened in May of 2009 and the Men's Health Club is thankfully on the first floor, with no steps to navigate.

Every once in a while, we learn that funeral services will be held for so-and-so at such-and-such a time. That means, of course, that we have lost another member. It can be a bit depressing. That's why we battle back against the inevitable with gin games, humor, some exercise and an occasional game of pool.

Just about every Club member bitches about his health. Arthritis is the 900-pound gorilla in the room, seemingly touching everybody. You can hear the grunts and groans as the members slowly plop down agonizingly into their chairs or else rise very haltingly with a curse on their lips because they are trapped in the so-called "Golden Years." One of my friends said: "Castration is far too good for the son-of-a-bitch who thought up that expression. Tell me what the hell is golden about these years? Golden, my ass."

Of course, the arthritis sufferers all have their own ideas about which medicine is the best for their pain. Some like Tylenol. Some like Excedrin. Others prefer Aspirin. Others say: "It doesn't matter what the fuck you use. None of this shit works anyway." This is usually followed by complaints that the giant drug companies are royally screwing the public. On this point, everyone agrees.

Clipping coupons is very big with some Club members. This makes me laugh because many of the "coupon clippers" are extremely wealthy. They don't need to drive miles and miles to get a 10-cent discount on a tiny greasy hamburger. But they just can't resist the lure of saving a few pennies—of "beating the price." Somehow, it's all part of being Jewish. It's in our collective psyche. When we were poor kids, pennies were precious. And although we are now in our 60s, 70s and 80s, we still cling to the old ways.

The gin games at the Club are what I look forward to the most. Although we don't play for big money, the competition is absolutely fierce and the players are generally excellent. They know how to play their hands properly. And they know better than to take advice from the many kibitzers (the self-proclaimed experts) who always watch the hands.

And a little light needling is always part of the action. One of the better players shouts "gingerbread" at his opponent just before he gins. "Can you stand a knock?" he asks at the very moment that he does knock, which means you are in big trouble if you are caught with a bunch of high cards in your hand.

The gin games seemingly go on forever. One reason is that many of the players have "frequency" and they have to rush to the john to relieve their bladders. They all say the same thing: "I'll be right back." And eventually, the game continues. (The sprint to the bathroom, by the way, is yet another "delight" that we can attribute to those "Golden Years.")

As I near the end of my life, I am grateful to God for giving me the family that I will always love and cherish deeply. I am also grateful that I was in a financial position to help other human beings who were in great need.

Finally, I am proud of the fact that this ghetto-kid, this high school dropout, this former janitor was able to rise above all obstacles and make his mark in the world.

And like the line in the classic Sinatra song: "I did it my way." CU

GONE BUT NOT FORGOTTEN

What some of my close friends might have said if they were still alive.

From Comedian Red Buttons (1919–2006): *"Ben, you were a great friend. I only wish I could have read your book. I only wish I could read any book. Of all 'the people who never had a dinner,' you were the most deserving. P.S. A word of advice: When your time comes, don't forget to bring along an electric blanket because it's colder than hell down here."*

From Comedian George Jessel (1898–1981): *"Ben, I'm passing time and staying busy by reading your terrific book. Many thanks for the $3,000 you gave me when I was down and out. Look what fast women and slow horses will do to a man."*

From former U.S. Senator Hubert H. Humphrey (1911–1978): *"Ben, I always enjoyed being in the company of you and your lovely wife, Marilyn. I wish you good luck with your book, and please don't forget to tell Nixon (wherever he may be) to return the large campaign donation you gave him. He told the nation he 'was not a crook.' What a crock."*

From the Hebrew School Rabbi I punched out: *"Ben, God and I forgive you for punching me in my beard. By the way, you hit pretty hard for a 12-year old kid. I'm glad to see that you have helped out hundreds of people over the years. That's a real mistsva."*

From Shig Katayama (1925–2007): *"Fixman, fuck your book. Just kidding. I really loved it, especially that chapter titled, 'The Jew and the Jap.' We truly were before our time as the business world's first odd couple. And thanks for delivering my eulogy. I greatly enjoyed listening to it. I need a favor. Please get me a subscription to the* Daily Racing Form. *It'll help me pass the time by analyzing the races. I can't tell you how much I miss the track and all the action, plus visiting the winner's circle. By the way, the next time I see you I will tell you about some great business ventures I have thought up. We'll make a pile of big bucks. It'll be just like the old days."*

PRESIDENTS, SENATORS AND
THE CONGRESSIONAL RECORD

Presidents? They are all the same. Send them some big bucks and back come some smiling photos and invitations. Politics—what a con game!

Citizens for Johnson and Humphrey

and

The President's Club of New York

cordially invite you to the

President's Ball

honoring

President and Mrs. Lyndon Baines Johnson

Saturday evening, June third

Nineteen hundred and sixty-seven

Cocktails at seven-thirty o'clock

Dinner at nine o'clock

Grand Ballroom

The Waldorf-Astoria

The Inaugural Committee
requests the honor of your presence
to attend and participate in the Inauguration of

Richard Milhous Nixon

as President of the United States of America
and

Spiro Theodore Agnew

as Vice President of the United States of America
on Monday the twentieth of January
one thousand nine hundred and sixty-nine
in the City of Washington

J. Willard Marriott
Chairman

January 20, 1969

In honor of

The Vice President-Elect of the United States and Mrs. Agnew

The Inaugural Committee

requests the honor of your presence at a

Reception

Sunday afternoon, the nineteenth of January

One thousand nine hundred and sixty-nine

five to eight o'clock

Smithsonian Institution, Museum of History and Technology

in the

City of Washington

Louise Gore
Charles S. Bresler
Co-Chairmen of the Vice President-Elect
Reception Committee

J. Willard Marriott
Chairman Inaugural Committee

*Invitation for
Richard M. Nixon's
Inauguration.*

Invitation for Ronald Reagan's Inauguration.

Mr. Ben Fixman -

With deepest appreciation for your generosity,

Ronald Reagan

THE BEN FIXMAN STORY:

Dear Mr. Fixman,

**Thanks to you, we received more votes than any other election in history.
God bless you all, God bless America.**

Congressional Record

United States of America

PROCEEDINGS AND DEBATES OF THE 92^d CONGRESS, FIRST SESSION

| Vol. 117 | WASHINGTON, THURSDAY, NOVEMBER 11, 1971 | No. 171 |

Senate

S 18222

AMERICAN JEWISH COMMITTEE HONORS MR. BEN FIXMAN WITH THE NATIONAL HUMAN RELATIONS AWARD

Mr. HUMPHREY: Mr. President, I recently had the fortunate experience of attending a most moving and inspiring event in St. Louis, a dinner to honor one of America's truly great citizens, Mr. Ben Fixman.

The evening was a moving one because of the fine statement of personal commitment to humanity, which Mr. Fixman presented.

And I found the evening inspiring because it was a warm demonstration by the sponsoring group, the American Jewish Committee, of its leadership since 1906 in combating bigotry and advancing the cause of human rights for all.

To be recognized for humanitarian leadership by the American Jewish Committee, Mr. President, is a high honor, indeed. Founded in 1906 to protect the civil and religious rights of Jews in the United States and abroad, then particularly against the oppression of Czarist Russia, the American Jewish Committee has fought to protect the enjoyment of human rights of all people in nearly ever forum and every battle. And the American Jewish Committee has always had in its leadership the most distinguished humanitarians.

I think Senators will appreciate a brief review of the history of the AJC, so I ask unanimous consent that there be printed at this point in the RECORD a chronological summary of its leadership and a list of its present officers and the names and terms of service of its presidents.

There being no objection, the summary was ordered to be printed in the RECORD, as follows:

MILESTONES OF THE AMERICAN JEWISH COMMITTEE
1906

Czarist Russia's oppression of Jews spurs creation of American Jewish Committee to protect the civil and religious rights of Jews in the United States and abroad. Founding leaders—men such as Dr. Cyrus Adler, Jacob H. Schiff, Cyrus L. and Mayer Sulzberger and Louis Marshall —vow to "alleviate the consequences of persecution and to afford relief from calamities affecting Jews wherever they may occur."

Within months of its establishment, the Committee had helped rebuild Jewish institutions leveled by earthquakes in San Francisco and Sicily and initiated plans for mass protest against Russian anti-Semitism.

1907-13

AJC assumes responsibility for preparing *American Jewish Year Book*, the standard, authoritative record of events and trends in world Jewish life.

AJC opposes discriminatory and restrictive immigration policies of U.S.

Four-year fight-led by Louis Marshall—opposing Czarist Russia's discrimination against Americans of Jewish faith results in U.S. abrogation of 1832 Russo-American Treaty of Commerce, Integrity of American citizenship vindicated.

Amendment to New York Civil Rights Law, supported by AJC, prohibits advertisement hotels and other public places. Other states later follow suit.

1914-20

Following outbreak of World War I, AJC provides relief for isolated Palestine Jews and plays major role in creation of Joint Distribution Committee for rescuing Jewish war victims in Europe.

Upon U.S. entry into the war, AJC leaders help create National Jewish Welfare Board to minister to needs of Jewish members of the armed forces.

New immigration law—advocated by AJC—accepts Yiddish and Hebrew as languages in literacy tests for immigrants to U.S.

AJC endorses Balfour Declaration, to establish Palestine as Jewish homeland.

Committee delegation, led by Louis Marshall, plays leading role in Paris Peace Conference decision to include minority-rights provisions in peace treaties.

AJC exposes the spurious anti-Semitic Protocols of the Elders of Zion.

1923-27

AJC plea in Oregon school case before U.S. Supreme Court helps establish right of Catholic parents to send children to parochial schools and defeats discriminatory law passed under KKK influence.

AJC joins in emergency relief activities to alleviate plight of more than 10,000 Jews stranded in European ports in route to U.S. by sudden passage of U.S. Immigration Act of 1924, based on national-origin quotes.

AJC spurs enlargement of Jewish Agency for Palestine to include non-Zionists.

In letter to AJC President Louis Marshall, Henry Ford retracts anti-Semitic statements and publicly apologizes for slandering Jews by circulating *Protocols of the Elders of Zion*.

1933-40

AJC urges U.S. intervention to protect the civil and religious rights of Jews in Nazi Germany; exposes Nazi persecution of Jews and other minorities; aids refugees; presses educational campaign in U.S. to counteract anti-Semitism and Nazi propaganda.

AJC initiates public opinion polls on attitudes toward Jews in the U.S.

AJC issues *Contemporary Jewish Record*, a periodical of events and digest of opinion in Jewish life, later succeeded by Commentary magazine.

AJC establishes Library of Jewish Information to service individuals and organizations with objective information about Jews.

AJC opposes British White Paper restricting Jewish immigration to Palestine; pledges cooperation with Jewish Agency "to help bring about a just, equitable and workable solution to the present Palestine problem ..."

1944-45

AJC convenes conference of social scientists to chart unprecedented research at major universities into prejudice, its roots, its effects on personality. Committee thus pioneers recruitment of social sciences in combating intergroup hostilities and advancing human relations.

Chapter movement founded to strengthen and expand AJC constituency and community relations programs.

At UN founding conference in San Francisco, AJC delegation, led by Judge Joseph M. Proskauer and Jacob Blaustein, helps secure inclusion of human-rights clauses in UN Charter.

AJC inaugurates *Commentary* magazine, a journal of independent thought and opinion on Jewish affairs and contemporary issues.

1946-47

AJC President Proskauer, at Anglo-American Committee of Inquiry, urges admission of 100,000 DP's to Palestine.

AJC supports Palestine partition plan.

AJC, Alliance Israelite Universalle and Anglo-Jewish Association form Consultative Council of Jewish Organizations, accredited to the UN, to safeguard rights of Jews, and human rights generally.

AJC opens European headquarters in Paris to help protect rights of Jews in Europe and North Africa, speed their integration, strengthen communal life.

AJC files brief in U.S. Supreme Court on released-time program. Court bars religious instruction in public schools.

AJC and Anglo-Jewish Association of Great Britain sponsor London Conference on needs of Jews in postwar Europe.

AJC delegation led by Jacob Blaustein, at Paris Peace Conference, successfully advocates human-rights guarantees and restitution provisions in peace treaties.

1948-50

AJC establishes office in Buenos Aires to help protect rights of Jews in Latin America. Program supports democratic institutions and fosters integration of Jews into Latin American communities.

AJC President Blaustein urges U.S. recognition of Israel.

In U.S. Supreme Court, AJC opposes enforcement of racial restrictive covenants. Court's ruling is first victory against such covenants.

Premier Ben-Gurion and AJC President Blaustein, in historic meeting, agree on principle that "Israel represents and speaks only in behalf of its own citizens [and] has no intention to interfere in any way in the internal affairs of Jewish communities abroad."

AJC-sponsored five-volume *Studies in Prejudice* (Harper & Brothers) is hailed by nation's social scientists. *The Authoritarian Personality*, basic volume in the series, has stimulated more than 1,000 further studies.

1951-52

Publication of AJC's *Jews in the Soviet Union* (Syracuse University Press) marks first exposure of Soviet anti-Semitism. Second volume, *Jews in the Soviet Satellites*, follows two years later.

AJC President Blaustein plays vital role in negotiation of $822,000,000 restitution settlement with Federal Republic of Germany in behalf of Israel and Conference on Jewish Material Claims against Germany; similar agreement is negotiated with Austria two years later.

AJC files brief in U.S. Supreme Court to stop state courts from granting damages for breach of racial restrictive covenants. Court affirms Committee's stand.

1954-55

AJC delegation, led by President Irvin M. Engel, surveys problems confronting 500,000 Jews of Morocco, Algeria and Tunisia; Committee fights for their right to choose citizenship with full equality, as well as to emigrate unhindered.

Committee brief in Supreme Court and AJC-sponsored research on effect of prejudice on personality contribute to decision banning school segregation.

AJC co-sponsors second London Consultative Conference of Jewish Organizations to determine program for insuring Jewish continuity in Western Europe and North Africa, and to discuss relation of Jews there to Israel.

1956-58

President Engel urges U.S. action to end discrimination by Arab

League nations against citizens of Jewish faith.

Pioneering AJC "Riverton Study" reveals attitudes of Jews toward themselves and their neighbors.

Pope Pius XII, addressing AJC delegation in his first private audience with a Jewish group, urges nations to provide haven for refugees fleeing persecution; condemns racial and religious persecution.

Ground is broken for Institute of Human Relations, AJC's permanent headquarters and hub for research and practical application in human relations.

With Anglo-Jewish Association and Alliance Israelite Universalle, AJC launches Community Service program in Europe to foster religious, cultural and educational cooperation among Jewish communities.

1959-60

AJC leaders meet in New York with Soviet Deputy Premier Mikoyan to protest situation of Soviet Jewry.

Week-long series of conferences, attended by more than 200 leading Americans, marks dedication of AJC's Institute of Human Relations.

Studies of "executive suite" discrimination in American industry are initiated by AJC at Harvard University Graduate School of Business, University of Michigan and University of California at Los Angeles Graduate School of Business.

AJC stimulates program which brings teams of West German educators to study U.S. teaching methods in education for democracy. Project continues in cooperation with West German Government, Institute of International Education, Ford Foundation, New World Foundation.

1961-62

Premier Ben-Gurion and Jacob Blaustein, in a joint statement, strongly reaffirm their 1950 understanding on relations between Israel and American Jews.

AJC submits to Vatican Council three memoranda, covering image of the Jew in Catholic teaching and liturgy, and suggesting ways to relieve religious tensions between Catholics and Jews.

AJC's Buenos Aires office mobilizes Argentine community and religious leaders to fight mounting anti-Semitism.

Faith and Prejudice (Yale University Press) reports findings of seven-year Yale Divinity School study, in cooperation with AJC, examining bias in Protestant teaching materials.

AJC opens office in Israel to help interpret the U.S. to Israel and clarify relationship between Israel and Jews in other lands.

President Kennedy confers with AJC delegation on wide range of human rights issues.

1963-64

AJC welcomes Augustin Cardinal Bea—one of the main architects of the Vatican Council resolution condemning anti-Semitism— to Institute of Human Relations. Pope Paul VI, in audience with AJC delegation, praises Committee's work.

AJC accords civil rights top program priority, convenes 125 business and industrial leaders for Washington meeting on responsibility of industry in race relations.

AJC's exposure of discriminatory patterns in utility industry spurs major U.S. Corporations to eliminate discrimination in the "executive suite."

Three-year Catholic self-study of bias in religious texts—encouraged by AJC— completed at St. Louis University.

AJC President Morris B. Abram exposes anti-Semitic Soviet publication; world-wide protest causes its withdrawal.

AJC leaders complete three-week fact-finding mission to Latin

America; report on anti-Semitism in Argentina, situation of Jews in Brazil, Chile and Peru.

1965-66

AJC hails Vatican Council declaration on Jews as "an act of justice long overdue," starts implementation program that includes institutes on Judaism at Catholic schools, conferences on changes in religious texts and interreligious dialogues in the local community.

AJC asks U.S. Government to insist that companies holding Government contracts end religious discrimination in filling top-management jobs.

AJC initiates pilot workshops in police-community relations. New York Police Commissioner and top officers attend first meeting at Institute of Human Relations.

AJC reveals virtual absence of Jews at administrative levels in U.S. colleges and universities. Report calls for end to bias.

AJC announces study at Louvain University, Belgium, of French-language Catholic religious materials used by 60 million people throughout the world.

Discrimination barring Jews from executive positions in savings and commercial banks is hit by AJC report.

1967-68

AJC helps mobilize American public opinion in behalf of Israel's security during Middle East crisis; moves to relieve plight of Jews in Arab countries; transfers office in Israel to Jerusalem and inaugurates human relations project there seeking better Jewish-Arab relations.

AJC Lakeville studies profile attitudes of Jews in suburbia toward their own identity and to Christians.

AJC moves to help implement major recommendations of Kerner

Report on causes of civil disorders; spurs efforts to provide jobs, education, housing for urban poor.

AJC sharply condemns anti-Semitic policies in Poland; continues to focus world public opinion on fate of Soviet Jews.

Nationwide study prepared for AJC on apostasy among college students.

AJC announces establishment of Oral History Library to chronicle modern American Jewish history.

1969-70

AJC sponsors major interfaith dialogues with Baptists, Lutherans, Presbyterians.

Executive Suite program to open management posts to Jews and members of other minorities expanded to all major industries in U.S.

Shaping Safer Cities program launched aimed at security without repression in major urban areas.

AJC launches nationwide program to meet needs of ethnic white minorities and counteract efforts of race-baiters.

AJC inaugurates community programs to reform welfare systems; embarks on local activities to meet needs of Jewish poor.

1971

AJC plays a pivotal role in organizations of protests and free-world action in defense of rights of Soviet Jews. AJC leaders confer with President Nixon, high administration officials. Worldwide reaction to trials of Jews in Leningrad leads to commutation of death sentences.

National Project on Ethnic America receives two-year Ford Foundation grant for new action projects for white working-class ethnic Americans.

Permanent interreligious consultation is organized between Vatican officials and International Jewish Committee on Inter-religious Consultations, of which AJC is constituent. Action follows similar permanent consultation arranged with World Council of Churches.

AJC focuses major world attention on long-standing anti-Jewish content of *Oberammergau Passion Play*, pledges 10-year effort to effect changes by 1980.

PRESIDENTS OF THE AMERICAN JEWISH COMMITTEE
Mayer Sulzberger, 1906-1912.
Louis Marshall, 1912-1929.
Cyrus Adler, 1929-1940.
Sol M. Stroock, Jan.-Sept. 1941.
Maurice Wertheim, 1941-1943.
Joseph M. Proskaues, 1943-1949.
Jacob Blaustein, 1949-1954.
Irving M. Engel, 1954-1959.
Herbert B. Ehrmann, 1959-1961.
Frederick F. Greenman, Apr.-June 1961.
Louis Caplan, 1961-1962.
A.M. Sonnabend, 1962-1964.
Morris B. Abram, 1964-1968.
Arthur J. Goldberg, 1969-1970.
Philip E. Hoffman, 1970-.

OFFICERS
Philip E. Hoffman, President.

BOARD CHAIRMEN
Max M. Fisher, National Executive Council.
David Sher, Board of Governors.

James Marshall.

William Rosenwald.

Maurice Glinert, Honorary Treasurer.

John Slawson, Executive Vice-President Emeritus.

MR. HUMPHREY: Mr. President, Mr. Fixman richly deserved this award and he presented to those in attendance a most moving statement of personal commitment to humanity.

Mr. President, I ask unanimous consent that there be printed at this point in the RECORD excerpts from the program of the dinner including the citation for the presentation of the 1971 Human Relations Award to Mr. Fixman.

There being no objection; the items were ordered to be printed in the RECORD, as follows:

The American Jewish Committee Appeal for Human Relations cordially invites you to attend a dinner marking the presentation of its National Human Relations Award to Ben Fixman, chairman of the board, Diversified Industries, Inc.

Keynote Address – Senator Hubert H. Humphrey.

Dinner Chairman – Morris A. Shenker.

Toastmaster – George Jessel.

Distinguished Guests – Senator Thomas F. Eagleton, Congressman James W. Symington.

Sunday, October 31, 1971, Chase-Park Plaza Hotel, St. Louis, MO.

The American Jewish Committee: Philip E. Hoffman, President; David Sher, Chairman, Board of Governors; Max M. Fisher, Chairman, Executive Council; and Elmer L. Winter, Chairman, Board of Trustees.

Previous Award Recipients: Willard F. Rockwell, Jr., Chairman of the Board, North American Rockwell Corp.; Edgar B. Speer, President,

United States Steel Corp.

Founded in 1906, the American Jewish Committee combats bigotry and advances the cause of human rights for all. Its national headquarters in New York is the Institute of Human Relations, a worldwide center for research, training and action for intergroup relations. It has an extensive overseas service with offices in Paris, Rio de Janeiro, Buenos Aires, Sao Paulo, Mexico City and Jerusalem and correspondents in many other cities.

In the United States, it has chapters and units in 100 principal cities and members in more than 600 American localities. Twenty-three regional offices throughout the country carry out AJC programs in cooperation with local community relations groups. The Committee is an accredited, non-governmental agency to the United States Mission to the United Nations.

The American Jewish Committee is privileged to present its 1971 Human Relations Award to Ben Fixman, a distinguished industrialist whose career has been marked by an abiding desire to help his fellow human beings.

In his rise from impoverished beginnings to business and financial success, Ben Fixman has never forgotten the less fortunate or those in need of a helping hand. He views communal service as an obligation and philanthropy as a sacred trust. He was Chairman of the 1970 Jewish Federation Fund Drive in St. Louis. He is a member of the Advisory Committee of the American Jewish Committee's St. Louis Chapter. Among the other causes he had aided are State of Israel Bonds and the Anti-Defamation League of B'nai B'rith.

He and Mrs. Fixman have been honored for their communal leadership by B'nai B'rith and Bonds for Israel, and were awarded a citation from the State of Israel for their efforts on behalf of Jewish survival.

We of the American Jewish Committee are proud to honor this warm and compassionate humanitarian and to have his name linked with ours in the effort to drive prejudice from the works and heart of man. We present him with this award in the knowledge that men often emulate those whom they honor.

Andrew Goodman, *National General Chairman, Appeal for Human Relations.*

Robert J. Jacobson, *New York Chairman, Appeal for Human Relations.*

MR. HUMPHREY: Mr. President, as I said in my own remarks, Mr. Fixman epitomizes the sense of civic consciousness and personal commitment which is essential if we are to make progress in solving the crucial questions facing our society today. Mr. Fixman's personal account of how he moved from the position of one persecuted to a greater defender of the persecuted deserves reading by every concerned American. I ask unanimous consent that Mr. Fixman's address be printed at this point in the RECORD.

SPEECH BY MR. BEN FIXMAN

Mr. Chairman, Senator Humphrey, Senator Eagleton, Congressman Symington, Mayor Cervantes, Lt. Gov. Morris, Rabbi Rubin, Rabbi Lipnick, our great Toastmaster, George Jessel, distinguished guests and friends:

Tonight I want to talk about people—people from all walks of life—people who show a deep concern for humanity and some people who couldn't care less about others. Be it good or bad ... this is human relations—this is what it's all about. In our lifetime, we have all seen human relations from both sides of the fence. We have seen men try to help others and we have seen men try to destroy others.

So, I ask myself tonight, what makes a man reach out to touch other men … to bring hope and purpose into their lives? What makes a man understand the needs of other people? What makes a man feel compassion toward other people, a compassion born not of pity, but a compassion that motivates a man to act for the betterment of other men?

I think it is somewhat of a paradox that the man you are looking at now—the man who so proudly and humbly accepts this Human Relations Award – was so injured by acts of inhuman relations that as a young man he was forced to hide the very thing he treasures most today —his religious heritage.

My life is a story of a deep and profound change in outlook. The reason for this change can be summed up in two sentences taken from the Talmud: "If I am not for myself, who is for me? And if I am only for myself, what am I?"

In my early years, I was far more concerned about the first question than the second. The world of my boyhood was a world of rampant bigotry … a world in which many families experienced bitter poverty … lack of education … and perhaps worst of all … constant gnawing fear —all because of their race, color or creed.

My family was such a family. We lived through hard times and we experienced in our own bodies and souls the ravages of prejudice and the anguish caused by man's inhumanity to man. These terrible experiences led me to become a member of what I call the "Invisible Minority" … these were people of my faith who tried to escape the afflictions of anti-Semitism by hiding their religious heritage. Without deliberately planning it and without stopping to analyze what I was doing … I took the safe, easy, convenient way out. And, so I thought of those two Talmudic questions again: "If I am not for myself, who is for me? And if I am only for myself, what am I?" As a young man, I was for myself. I answered the first question without ever stopping to consider the consequences of the second.

Many times since then, I have looked back on my early experiences and wondered why I acted as I did. What force motivated me to emerge from the hidden depths of this invisible minority? What made me stand up and say I am a Jew? And I think I have the answer. I now know that deep down inside himself, every person must exist in his own identity or he cannot exist at all – whether he be Catholic, Jew, Protestant, Black or White. So, I finally learned from my own experience that a person who has pride in himself can respect pride in others. I know the answer to that question in the Talmud. "If I am only for myself, what am I?" My friends, the answer is obvious, nothing.

I would like to tell you a heartbreaking story that I can never forget. At the end of World War II, when Allied troops were sweeping through Germany, some GI's entered a basement of a home in the City of Cologne to see if any Nazis were hiding there. They didn't find the enemy, but they did uncover an unforgettable inscription on the walls of this basement, which turned out to be a hiding place for Jews … a place where terrified families tried to escape from the troops who filled the streets above. Sometime during those grim years before 1945, an unknown Jew had written these three sentences on the cellar wall:

"I believe in the sun even when it is not shining."

"I believe in love even when not feeling it."

"I believe in God even when he is silent."

For many of us … for the Jews living in the Soviet Union … for the Hungarian Freedom Fighters … for the valiant Czechoslovakians … for the Blacks and impoverished people who live in our ghettos … for many of these people, the sun has never shone in their lifetime … love has not been felt very often … and God has seemed to hide his face. Instead of sunshine, they have encountered ominous clouds … and instead of love, they have felt maniacal hatred. But despite all of this, they will never stop believing. Therefore, we are often inspired by the man who rises from the depths of great adversity through his heroism and faith.

We must all believe. We must try to translate our belief into compassion. We must try to remember the common humanity that unites us all.

Why do some men judge other men not by what they are, but by their race, religion or their background? Why do some men judge other men by the way they talk or the way they dress? And there are those who judge men only by what they have in their pockets and not in their hearts.

I prefer to judge men by their deeds, not their backgrounds. I look at men and women of accomplishment and see only men and women. My friends are my friends. Having a certain religious belief was never a condition of my friendship.

In the past 10 years, the main thrust of my efforts has been directed toward helping the State of Israel. Let us deal with human relations as it applies to this country. Here we have a nation of three million people drawn from all parts of the world all having come to this desert wasteland to make a better life for themselves and their families and to live in peace.

Even though they have lived almost continually in the shadow of wars and death, these valiant people have offered their Arab neighbors the benefit of their technical knowledge to better their education, to improve their medical facilities, to find jobs and to raise the efficiency of their backward industries.

How often in history has a conqueror so surrounded by blood enemies offered an olive branch of peace and said: "Come let us share and grow together."

This is truly human relations at its finest.

Without Israel, the plight of those Jews who hid in that basement in Cologne becomes a mockery. Without Israel, all our noble words about human relations become ashes in our mouths. And I repeat what Senator Humphrey said, For without Israel, there is no Democratic government in the Middle East.

My goal, my dream is to contribute to a world of better human relations—a world which has been enriched by actions of men and women like yourselves—people who have dedicated their lives to creating a better understanding between all religions, all races and all nations.

This is the kind of world I want my children and your children and their children to grow up in.

Today, the words of those who advocate bigotry, hatred and prejudice are more often falling on deaf ears. Today in America, we hear the voices of the minorities and the oppressed. We are listening. We are acting. We are making progress. We will solve their problems. We must have faith in our country.

And so these are some of my thoughts tonight as I look back upon my years of working toward improving human relations. As I accept this award, I can only try—although I cannot possibly succeed—to tell you how humble I really feel. There are two reasons why:

One is that a Jew who practices good human relations is not really doing anything special—he is simply being in our tradition—a Jew.

The second reason is that this honor comes from the American Jewish Committee, an organization that actually deserves the award itself. For 65 years, the American Jewish Committee has fought for better human relations—it has battled to eliminate prejudice and bigotry—it has resisted every form of man's inhumanity to man—and it has never forgotten that in Judaism—religiousness is social action.

It may seem strange in an era that has seen Holocaust and genocide —to remain optimistic. It may seem strange—in a century that has seen massive persecutions—to remain hopeful. But that is what we must do. For we cannot lose hope—all of our faiths forbid it. In Judaism, despair is considered a grave sin—an affront to God and His creation. So let me close by repeating to you the words of a great but little known scholar. These words deserve to be engraved on the hearts of all men—prophetic words that give means and significance to life itself. And I quote: "I do not know what despair is. Despair means utter futility, being utterly lost. I will never be lost." And, so we must never lose hope—we must never give up.

But to make improved human relations a fact of life, all of us in this room have a very hard task ahead. And this task was summed up very appropriately in the words of Charles DeGaulle who said:

"We have been to the moon, but that really isn't very far … for the greatest distance we have to cover still lies within ourselves."

Thank you.

MR. HUMPHREY: Finally, Mr. President, I ask that my remarks of the evening in tribute to this great American and his leadership be printed in the RECORD.

There being no objection, the remarks were ordered to be printed in the RECORD, as follows:

REMARKS OF SENATOR HUBERT H. HUMPHREY HONORING BEN FIXMAN

I have come here tonight to honor one of St. Louis' great civic leaders and a great family. In his capacity as a leading industrialist and citizen, Ben Fixman has well earned the National Human Relations Award. It is an honor richly deserved. I personally view this award with great respect because it represents a crowning effort on the part of a single individual to generate the kind of citizen responsibility which can make this country pulsate with vitality and renew our sense of justice and decency.

What disturbs me is that there is not enough of this kind of personal commitment nationwide. It's so needed.

I will always be eternally grateful for Senator Hubert Humphrey, center, for placing my speech in the Congressional Record. Missouri Senator Tom Eagleton, left, joined Senator Humphrey and I in the celebration.

It is this sense of civic consciousness and personal commitment that motivates me to discuss with you what I think are some of the crucial questions facing our society today—questions on which the work of the American Jewish Committee and B'nai B'rith have concentrated their activities for so long and so well.

As I see it, each one of us should have at least three levels of concern in our relations with other human beings.

First, each one of us should be concerned with the welfare of those people affecting him the most—his family, friends, and the city in which he lives. But is he?

He should be concerned with the future of his country—the human progress of American society. But is he?

He should be concerned as a citizen of the world with the whole human family—the social and economic condition of human beings everywhere? But is he?

There was a time when my answers to all these questions would have been in the affirmative. I thought that every city, and every country was blessed with Ben Fixman. I still think they are. But now I am less certain that there are enough of them to go around. And I am less convinced that our own government or any contemporary government has taken full advantage of them.

Perhaps, in our race for technological gains, we have forgotten what society is all about—the people—their welfare—their safety and their freedom.

In a Gallup poll undertaken for a comparative study of American public opinion by the International Institute for Social Research, a cross-section of the American public expressed a new and urgent concern over where our country, our society was going—concern for the future. It was found that there was a pervasive sense of national worry and fear that the nation was disunited and its institutions were unresponsive to the needs of people. The study concludes, and I quote, "Americans sense that their country has lost rather than gained ground over the past five years." The recurrent explanation?—"Our traditional way of doing things is not working and some basic changes are needed if we are to work together."

There is a deep and profound gap between ideals and reality. There is glowing rhetoric about all the people and yet neglect of so many people; job opportunity, and yet so much unemployment; wealth and yet so much human poverty; justice, and yet so many social inequities, economic development, and yet the dwindling of foreign economic assistance.

We have serious troubles.

Our economy is lagging and unemployment stays around 6 percent. Discriminatory practices against racial and ethnic groups still deny many Americans equal opportunities for self-development. Our government on the federal and local levels has not yet responded imaginatively to the urgent needs.

Where are the programs for hunger, poverty, unemployment, health, poor housing, and inadequate education? We have a huge defense budget, and a spiraling arms race. Peace is still not within our reach, not when there is Vietnam, Pakistan, and the Middle East.

The subject of foreign aid and the U.N. has again become news. The entire legislative history of foreign aid has shown that it has always been difficult to get passage of these measures. This problem becomes more acute in times of domestic economic difficulty and recession. When the Congress is concerned with the lack of jobs and rising inflation, the passage of a foreign aid bill requires delicate and full cooperation between the Executive branch and the legislative leadership. Yet, what has been the case in this instance?

We find the President maintaining little or no contact with the Congressional leadership for over several weeks prior to action on the bill. Then, when the Administration did give a nod to the Congress regarding the foreign aid bill, it was a "scruff of the neck, back of the hand" approach, wherein the President held up to the Senate the threat of a veto if the bill should contain any amendments which he did not want. This coupled with the President's intemperate remarks following the ouster of Nationalist China from the United Nations put fuel on the fires of neo-isolationism. The President's threats to those liberal members of the Senate who wished to assure no further expansion of our war efforts in Indo China coalesced with his harsh statements against the United Nations, to defeat this foreign aid bill.

But, there will be American aid—we cannot retreat from responsibility —we cannot refuse aid to refugees, to economic development, the U.N., to Israel.

To possess the goal of peace does not produce its realization anymore than the ideal of justice and freedom brings its instantaneous accomplishment. The Middle East is a case in point. Here is an example of the human dilemma. The seemingly insurmountable gap between the idea and reality. Israel's requests are modest—a right to live in peace— certainly, a reasonable goal for any nation. Yet because of Arab hostility, a lack of understanding and intolerance, that goal has so far proved illusory. Israel has been fighting for its life—its right to live, to be free and independent, to develop its physical and human resources. Let Israel know we care. Let the Soviets know we care.

The Middle East is a powder keg with a very short fuse, ready to explode if any one of the participants strikes the match of revived hostility. While the Middle East conflict began as a confrontation between the Arab countries and Israel, it now threatens to spark a confrontation between the two powerful nuclear Goliaths of the earth, the United States and the Soviet Union.

For the hope of peace to become a reality, the United States must be steadfast. We must assure that Israel is well equipped with the defensive weapons necessary to deter any attack. A balance of power in that part of the world provides the kind of stability which is ultimately conducive to reaching a negotiated settlement. The prospect of peace through negotiation is jeopardized when our government refuses or delays to act on Israel's request for Phantom jets and other badly needed economic and military assistance.

I mentioned the ideals of justice and freedom, but what do they mean when persecution of a religious minority is on the rise in the Soviet Union and when we at home still face the unfinished business of almost two centuries—the task of securing full rights of citizenship and human dignity for all races and creeds.

In the Soviet Union today, there is an organized effort to suppress an entire Jewish community. The systematic assault on their dignity and their freedom is not a problem for Russian Jews alone—nor a problem only for Jews.

It is a situation in which the United States should use official channels in an attempt to curb the persecution, and permit the right of Soviet Jewry to emigrate to any land. It is an example of the kind of human bond I have been talking about, hoping for, and seeking my entire life to secure.

It is certainly plausible that our country and individual Americans can do a great deal to pressure Soviet leaders. I myself am doing what I can through personal and official channels and through legislation in the Senate, but more can be done. This government of ours and the American people should speak up for freedom wherever freedom is denied.

We should speak up for human dignity wherever people are victims of indignity and of humiliation.

We must do all we can to disarm the world of its prejudice and bigotry. This kind of disarmament needs to take place in America just as it does in the Soviet Union. This is the work of the American Jewish Committee.

We can close the gap between myth and reality. We can reshape the reality to restore the faith in our institutions. All this can be done and more, but the essential ingredient is leadership. That is what we need.

THEN & NOW

THEN — 18th and Carr, 1930

NOW — 18th and Carr, 2009

PARTIAL ARTICLE FROM THE *POST-DISPATCH*
DECEMBER 28, 1949:

FINDS ST. LOUIS' SLUMS AS BAD AS THEY COME

ST. LOUIS SLUMS ARE "AS BAD AS THEY COME," BUT THE CITY IS "AHEAD OF THE AVERAGE CITY IN PLANNING SLUM CLEARANCE AND LOW-COST HOUSING," A FEDERAL HOUSING OFFICIAL DECLARED HERE YESTERDAY AFTER A TOUR OF THE CRITICAL AREAS.

WARREN J. VINTON, FIRST ASSISTANT COMMISSIONER OF THE PUBLIC HOUSING ADMINISTRATION, CALLED ST. LOUIS' SLUM AREAS "JUST INHUMAN" AND TERMED THEM A THREAT TO DEMOCRACY. THERE CAN'T BE A CONTINUING DEMOCRACY, HE WARNED, "UNDER THOSE HOUSING CONDITIONS." HE URGED ST. LOUIS, IN DRAWING ITS IMMEDIATE PLANS, TO KEEP THE OVER-ALL SCHEME FOR TOTAL ELIMINATION OF THE SLUMS IN MIND.

EVERY CITY, HE ADDED, SHOULD HAVE A MINIMUM HOUSING STANDARDS LAW TO AVOID REPEATING THE SAME MISTAKES. PUBLIC HOUSING, HE SAID, SHOULD BE INTEGRATED INTO URBAN REDEVELOPMENT, AND LOW-INCOME HOUSING SHOULD BE MIXED WITH MIDDLE INCOME RATHER THAN STANDING ALONE.